To Randy & Wendy

Recollection and Reckoning: A Montana Childhood,

1949-1967

James Howard Trott

OAK AND YEW
PRESS

Oak and Yew Press

Recollection and Reckoning: A Montana Childhood,

1949-1967

James Howard Trott

Philadelphia

Oak and Yew Press

The author as a young cowboy.

TABLE OF CONTENTS

IN MEMORY – INTRODUCTION

If all of us were sculptors and our life were a series of reliefs or statuary, then accurate memory would be a room full of casts, ready to reproduce those original figures in the materials we think suitable. Memory re-casts some of these in gold, some in lead, some in mere clay. Some of the casts we would like to discard or try to destroy, yet somehow these very ones show up at the front of the shelves.

Memorials are the substantial statues, photos, or other material tokens which inspire memory in her more insubstantial re-castings. Often memorials, at least the public ones, have words engraved on them or plaques containing words, perhaps lists of names, or brief descriptions of historical events.

Today, on the internet we are regularly offered "memes," which are generally not so much memorials as propaganda – not so much oriented toward re-casting memories as re-shaping our interpretation of reality.

And at the same time a very ambitious enterprise encourages us to view all knowledge and memory as completely fluid, as bearing next to no connection to anything which might legitimately be called "reality". Thus post-modernism joins modern psychology in viewing memory essentially as a survival mechanism by which the individual protects him- or her-self, while at the same time, influencing as many others as possible. Memory seen thus, like language, is pure politics and power-play.

My earliest memories are two. In what must be the earliest (reserving some doubt) I stood tiptoe beside a hospital bed from which my Grandmother, Louise Gwinn Hanford, leaned to give me a kiss. With that objectification which memory so often insists upon, I can see it as almost a

1

photograph, with parents and others hovering in the background. But I can also see it as me, looking up at this nearly-sacred one who loved me. She died soon after that.

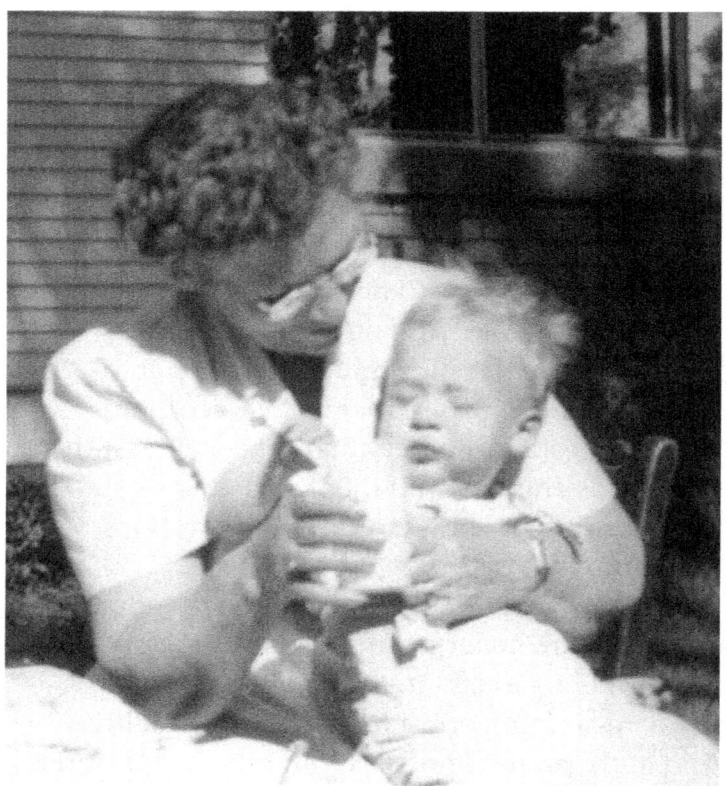

Grandmother holding me in the yard at 1904 Franklin.

My other early memory may be dated to when I was about four. (My memory cares little for chronology. I know some who seem to have a punch clock connected to theirs, and at times I envy them.)   It took place in the kitchen at 1904 Franklin Street in Fort Benton, Montana. My father had redone that kitchen for my mother and I have a dim version of what may be an earlier memory, in which he carefully cuts out original curlicues in green and brown to customize the squares of the linoleum floor. But on the occasion I am recounting, my mother sat on the red and white (Cosco) metal stool with the middle step that folded out to form a little stair, and I sat upon her lap. She said something, perhaps about how cozy we were, or perhaps what she said had little to do with my question to her, which was "Will I remember this when I grow up?" To which she replied, "You will if you want to, Jimmy." And I do.

Christmas card 1951.

Thus my early memories are on the theme of mortality, but also on the persistence of memory. The latter case seems also to be about memory as a servant of will. A great deal is often said about the transitory and unreliable nature (sometimes characterized as the fluidity) of memory. These observations tend to be "memes," things heard and repeated without a great deal of consideration or skepticism. This is unfortunate. Memory needs skepticism. Memories which are not viewed critically are like unsorted photographs.

Most of us recognize there is a kind of horror to the infinite multiplication of digital images which our technology now furnishes us the means for. If these are not severely sorted and a high percentage discarded, the next generation will discard them ALL. We will not end up with too much fuel for memory but NONE. Skeptical analysis and selection of memory and of photographs is itself a large part of our growth in knowledge, understanding, and wisdom. We compare photograph with photograph and determine which is better and develop criteria why these are better than those.

Family garbed for some commemoration or other, 1954.

The tools by which we record, collate, edit and discard – or preserve – memories are remarkable. I take them to be basic to the description of man as made in the image of God. Modern biology and psychology tend to devalue the incredible faculties of the human heart and mind – squeezing them all inside our skulls as animal functions of an organic brain bent on survival. But in an earlier book, *Poetry at the Heart of Things,* I outlined a much higher view of what the ancients called "the inward wits" in a discussion of the Imagination:

> There is grace for the right combination of resistance and submission amidst the world's paradigms – grace that leads to analysis and some measure of reconstruction in right imaginings. This is more of a community project than an individual one. . .
>
> . . .We have thus far used the term "fancy" as a negative term, denoting a debased imagination. But fancy has at times also been distinguished from imagination as a positive "wit" – and the term was sometimes used this way in earlier literature. Therefore those schooled in the earlier literatures – such as C.S. Lewis, J. R. R. Tolkien, and Dorothy Sayers, sometimes use it in this positive sense.
>
> . . .In his *Studies in Words,* (during his discussion of the word "sense") C. S. Lewis describes Medieval psychology as distinguishing ten "wits," that is five "inward wits" as well as five "outward wits". The outward wits are our familiar "five senses," but the five inward wits are memory, estimation, fancy, imagination, and common wit. The last of these is "common sense," which does not so much mean "common to men," as "unifying," that is, functioning to coordinate the individual's other wits. Lewis quotes [Robert] Burton, writing that "common wit or common sense" :

> > . . .is the judge or moderator of the rest, by whom we discern all differences of objects; for by mine eye I know not that I see, or by mine ear that I hear, but by my common sense.

Although Lewis quotes Burton in regard to the inward wits, Burton seems to have only distinguished three inward wits, where Lewis finds five referred to by other writers. Burton's three are Common Sense, Memory, and Phantasy (which he does not distinguish from imagination, and he may include estimation here as well). . . .

> Phantasy, or imagination . . .is an inward sense which doth more fully examine the species perceived by common sense, of things present or absent, and keeps them longer, recalling them to mind again or making new of his own. In time of sleep this faculty is free, and many times conceives strange, stupend, absurd shapes, as in sick men we commonly observe. . . .[phantasy's or imagination's] objects [are] all the species communicated to him by common sense, by comparison of which he feigns infinite others to himself. In melancholy men this faculty is most powerful and strong, and often hurts, producing many monstrous and prodigious things, especially if it be stirred up by some terrible object . . . from common sense or memory. In Poets and Painters imagination forcibly works as appears by their several fictions, anticks, images: as Ovid's House of Sleep, Psyche's Palace in Apuleius, &c.

To my modern mind, memory seems out of place among the "inward wits". I think this is because we have come to regard memory mechanically – largely through the analogy of computer "memory". Yet when we think about it, memory is an active, associative, comparative and even analytic faculty, a "wit" indeed.

The distinction of estimation, fancy, and imagination as separate faculties deserves more study.

Estimation in particular is worthy of study: the ability
to come to a preliminary understanding while
conscious one's knowledge is incomplete. I suppose it's
oriented toward concrete more than abstract things, but
this again may be due to our contemporary usage.

The term "Fantasy" comes from Greek "*phaino,* "
having to do with appearance, visibility. Appearance,
of course, has the potential to mean illusion – 'so it
appeared'. *Phanein* is to show or make visible. *Phanos*
is a lantern. Related English words are Phantom and
Fantastic. An old word for a boaster is "Fantast ".

So early in English, "fancy" meant imagination;
and later came to be used of delusive imagination (vain
imagination). Tolkien and Lewis liked the older
meaning, and so were happy to label some of their
work as fantasy literature. A work of George
MacDonald which deeply influenced Lewis early in his
Christian faith is titled *Phantastes*.

But we see the more negative usage in "David's
Peccavi" by Robert Southwell in the Sixteenth-century:

> I fancy deemed fit guide to leading my way,
> And as I deemed I did pursue her track;
> Wit lost his aim, and will was fancy's prey;
> The rebel won, the ruler went to wrack.
> But now sith fancy did with folly end,
> Wit bought with loss, will taught by wit, will
> mend.

As Burton mentioned, imagination or fantasy do
with memory and idea much the same things as happen
in dreams. But perhaps it is only/usually fantasy at
work in dream – for there is an inevitability and a
tediousness to dreams that seems contrary to the nature
of the best imagination. Yet many of us have had
memorable dreams that we can scarcely doubt are
parables or contain powerful metaphors with profound

meaning of value to us. In my own case, on perhaps ten occasions I have awakened from a dream with an immediate profound sense of the allegory. I knew exactly its application to me -- what God was saying to me through it. Of course on thousands of other occasions I've had no clue.

My imagination, or perhaps its improper use, makes me a poor witness. (I often "fancy" or imagine something to fill a gap in my actual knowledge.) It also makes me a very poor searcher. I can look carefully through a drawer several times before complaining to my wife that what I seek is not there, whereupon she takes a glance into the drawer and lifts out the object. I have come to this conclusion for my excuse: I picture the thing I seek too exactly – this side up, that color, etc., and expect it to appear in exact conformity to the image I have created. I am thus actually blindered from seeing the object where it lies by my expectation of how it should look. A properly imaginative approach (perhaps a more accurate "estimation," insofar as that faculty is distinguished) would leave room for a less-defined expectation, and allow me see the real thing.

Tolkien, "On Fairy Stories" gives his take on fancy and imagination. He sees imagination as the more mechanical faculty doing what I've just complained of -- producing images in the mind. He then puts "fancy" higher, making it the amalgamating or creative part. But he seems to know that he is taking a minority position on this. (He does not deal with the idea of destructive or detrimental imagination in his prose, but certainly there are prime examples of that in his *Lord of the Rings*!)

Florence Conway Williams ("Michal"), wife of Charles Williams, draws a parallel between the two relationships of an emblem (or sign) to a symbol – and of fancy to imagination. She says:

In parenthesis it may be remarked that t[
distinction between fancy and imaginati[
applicable to emblems and symbols. The first
deals with apparent likenesses, the second with
images made one with the thing they image, or
having the same essential idea. The first is
accidental, perhaps temporary; the second
necessary, perhaps eternal.

So again, we return to a distinction between
fancy and imagination, making the former more
"surfacy," the latter more profound. Florence Williams'
take is perhaps a good balance, and the terminology
less important than the realization that there is good
and bad use of imagination, no matter how we label it.
Augustine's principles that proper interpretation, and
thus expression, are to be guided by love and faith, will
be enough to maintain a right perspective.[1]

I have written one other book titled as a "memoir".[2] It
covers my involvement in what is generally called "the pro-life
rescue movement" over a period of nine years. In writing that
memoir I had to rack my memory at many points, but I also
went to printed and published sources of that period, to
personal records and letters, and to a particularly extensive
photographic record kept by one of my compatriots. I was
very selective toward the goal of giving a full and accurate
account of my experiences and the general thinking and
intentions of those I participated with, as well as bringing up
the more difficult dilemmas those experiences and thoughts
raised – expecting the reader to gain something which would
serve him or her in parallel situations.

---

[1] *Poetry At The Heart Of Things: Towards A Christian Perspective*, James Howard
Trott, Oak and Yew Press , Philadelphia, copyright 2016.
[2] *Was That Thunder? A Memoir Of Pro-life Rescue, 1988-1997*, James H. Trott,
Oak and Yew Press , copyright 2015.

I also had a double-goal of being as charitable as I felt appropriate when touching on various wrong-doers and their wrong-doing, while calling the reader to see our own complicity and need for wider national repentance in the greater evil of legalized abortion.[3]

The five inward senses must work together under the oversight of "common sense" if we are to do something well – and that includes remembering and communicating our memories to others.

My four youngest siblings and our dog Bart on the farm.

Accuracy in memory at times appears to be in inverse proportion to imagination or intelligence. The camera and tape recorder "remember" many things more accurately than the human being. Persons with very little imagination are often the very best witnesses. So far as I can tell, my own siblings, like me, are not always reliable as witnesses. We have exhibited a spectrum of misremembering that is itself rather

---

[3] *Was That Thunder?*

remarkable. We have a wide range of impressions as to who our parents were – what they were like, what "made them tick," and even some of the particular things they did and said. I have collected evidence from both sides of our family that the same was often true of the previous generation. The only surviving member of that generation, my Aunt Elizabeth, aunt by marriage, is still a more reliable witness at 98 years old than my father's siblings were – who had, for instance, radically different memories of the dynamics of their parents' marriage.

Our family has exhibited a variety of misrememberings including: 1/ A strange ability to "cast" different people in central roles in various events, even to the extent of "remembering" oneself in a role of a story others of us thought belonged to someone else. This extends to supporting roles, as well. 2/ To remember widely different settings as the locations and times in which various events transpired; and 3/ To attribute widely differing motives to central characters in past events. The last, of course, is more abstract, and lends itself to the varied perspectives of those doing the remembering.

But who did what to whom, how, when, and where, are ultimately matters of fact, postmodernism not withstanding. Among several versions of an event, one account is likely to be more accurate – although it is true, the blind men may be reporting accurately about respective parts of the elephant.

One can never be quite suspicious enough, or at all the right times, about one's own memory. But knowing that may help keep one humble and more accurate.

There will be stories in this memoir about things I did not witness at all, but only heard about from others. That's the point where memories become stories, perhaps to be judged as much as literature as history.

There is a powerful tradition of storytelling among humans in general, and in my family, in particular. My father and uncles, cousins and friends were all storytellers, and some of them master storytellers.

My grandparents, Louise and J. Arthur Hanford, -- and me.

There seemed to be a written rule something like the one in checkers that if you can jump an opponent, you have to. Well, the story-telling version was, if you have a story on the same subject or theme as the last fellow's, you have to tell it. This made for wonderful long sessions around the table after meals – especially on holidays when the best story-tellers were gathered. Similarly, I am propelled by the feeling that there are some good stories that need to be told.

But in the end both literature and history ought to point to abiding truth, and one ought to present it in such a way that the reader is glad of it.

As always the degree to which a writer succeeds at his stated goals must be judged by his readers, and thus I lay this "memoir" before the court -- the judge and jury is you.

RECOLLECTION AND RECKONING

There's a certain *hubris* that goes with writing a memoir – and in Greek tragedy *hubris* always leads to a tragic ending. Can I get away without setting myself up for a fall? The key seems to be something about keeping perspective on what our memories are for – what they teach. I've mentioned another memoir of mine which had to do with an important nine year period of my life. Partly because I saw so much of my own weakness during that time, I don't think it ended up piling much fuel on my *hubris*. My poetry is often bits and snatches of memoir – attempts to catch what is eternal in the moment, sometimes as haphazardly as flies are caught in amber. Some of my poetry is more hubristic, which means it's not good poetry. The flies were too artificially arranged.

Lucille and James Edwards Trott with Brother Pete and me.

It seems safe to suggest most fiction writers inculcate bits of disguised memoir in their work. Is it only now that I'm catching hints of how spotty and erratic my memory grows that I am moved to record what remains? Setting up guideposts against the fog, so to speak? The worst losses so far seem to be in the short term component, but time is fleeting and inevitably defeats the memory that pursues it.

As mentioned above, the idea of the five "inner wits," suggests memory functions in tandem with the other faculties. Beside these, there are short-term and long-term storerooms, and also different kinds of archives -- from the immediately available to the dusty dog-eared boxes buried under the pile, which can only be got at with a great deal of trouble, if at all. There are also cross-reference files in memory, for instance, the memory of 'to whom one has told what'.

I have friends who completely lack this cross-reference file – and will tell you the same thing ten times, given just a little time between. Of course there are excuses for milder forms of this – no one remembers exactly what he has told everyone else. My good friend Roger Custer and I worked together fairly steadily for six years and it got to where we told each other stories back and forth, to the point where every story seemed to have had been confirmed several times over. We do to some degree keep each other accountable in regard to our memories, but as in this case, group memory can be faulty, too.

I wonder, then, if a good memoir isn't more a series of stories than an historical document. Others will no doubt finds faults of fact in what one records, but a memoir is much more than facts. There is something mysterious and wonderful in the selectivity of memory. And those things which have been formulated into words on earlier occasions have developed, have accreted so to speak, and grown into something both universal and all their own.

I mentioned my very first memories above – the oldest events I can recall: standing next to my Grandmother's hospital bed and sitting on my mother's lap on a Cosco stool.

If I am honest, I must admit, it's extremely unlikely I knew it was a Cosco stool at the time. Memory seems to have priorities other than strict reporting – it would rather gather design, color and drama than arrange it all strictly by the calendar. Later elaborations are not forbidden.

Aunt Jean looks on as Mom takes a photo.

Photography has affected my memory, too. Both my parents were photo buffs – indeed my Dad was an Army Air Force photographer during WWII in Italy. My mother's aunts were photographers. Likewise, her four siblings, their spouses, and children. My brothers and I have worked to preserve the various forms of photographic record they kept (slides, 8mm movies, and prints). I scanned nearly 10,000 old photographs (four generations contributing) into digital form. Most of the photographs I have included in this memoir were taken by my mother and digitized by my brother Pete. Others were taken by relatives, by Dad, or me or by my other siblings.

Although it can be tedious, I have enjoyed editing them. That, too, informs memory.

But photos can have something of the same effect on memory as watching an old Disney version of some classic tale – overprinting Disney's idea of what the Seven Dwarfs looked like on my own imagination, only in this case there may be a bit closer correlation between my memory and photos of the actual events and people. A correlation, but not an exact match. I fear the photos often trump the memory. I love photography, finding something very satisfying in getting a good portrait of a wild bird or recording a wonderful sunset – formerly on film, now digitally. However, I also know enough to distrust it.

Both photographs and one's critical assessment of them help with the selections for a memoir. What has already been recorded in one medium need not be re-recorded. And the most avid photographer cannot possibly snap photos of most of life. In fact nearly always the best stories escape the photographer altogether.

Nonetheless just as others' memories help, so can photos. I have no recollection of many events which old photos record. These include my baby days, with their significant events -- some of which have no photo record either That then throws me back on others' memories.

For accounts of my birth I am wholly dependent on what I was told. My father was working with his brother-in-law Uncle Norris Hanford on his farm, learning the rudiments of that trade, which would become his chief vocation for the next thirty years. Although I think Mom and Dad were living in Fort Benton in an apartment in "The Hagen Block," Mom went out to the Hanford farm that day perhaps to help Aunt Dorothy with the harvest cooking, but also to be nearby should her imminent labor begin. As it indeed did, and when things had reached a certain pitch, Dorothy went out to tell Norris as he travelled back and forth from field to farmyard with the grain truck. Norris was hauling the new cut grain from the combine with which Dad was cutting it.

Norris drove out next to the combine in the field, signaling Dad to stop, then climbed up the ladder and over the racket of the combine shouted to Dad, "Lucille is ready," and that he would take over the combine.

As he dismounted, Dad remembered one important piece of information. He turned and hollered back through the racket, "the water-bag is in the grain tank!" This was due to the fact that a little earlier the canvas water-bag, which with its petroleum-flavored, but moderately cool water was a regular feature of tractor and combine driving up into my mid-teens, had broken its rope handle and tumbled down into the grain tank where the cut and threshed wheat was collecting. Norris smiled and waved Dad away on his rather important errand, although it turned out he didn't understand what Dad had said, and thought it was something inconsequential.

Dad drives combine as the water-bag hangs over the grain tank.

When Dad got to the farmyard, and walked up to the house, Mom came out carrying a swaddled baby in her arms – actually a baby-doll. These are the kind of jokers I was born to! They then headed up to Great Falls, where I, alone of my siblings was born. (The rest were born at St. Clare Hospital in Fort Benton.) Meanwhile Uncle Norris, probably with Aunt Dorothy as temporary truck driver, started to unload his load of wheat from the combine into the truck. But suddenly the auger on the combine came to a screeching halt (those drive belts did indeed screech when a pulley jammed), and Norris spent a good deal of the rest of the afternoon extricating the remains of the canvas water-bag from where it was lodged in the auger! Thus was my birth marked as memorable in more ways and by more persons than just my parents! I heard the details reiterated on several occasions by aunt, uncle and parents.

We rely on others for a large part of our story. For another instance, they tell me when I was a baby my parents left me quiet and cooing under the Christmas tree, and returned to find, to their horror that I had managed to get hold of a small glass ornament and bitten down on it, swallowing a few pieces of glass.   No serious complications resulted. However, I had an unusually low voice as a youngster. My vocal chords may have been affected by the event.

Christmases were huge events each year at our house. From the photos I know that as the first child of the youngest daughter in the greater Hanford clan, I was annually buried in presents. Among the most precious are a rocking horse my father and mother made – which many years later inspired me to make copies for my children's children. There are a few photos of my parents at work on that project and these warm my heart with a sense of continuity. There were many other homemade, as well as innumerable manufactured toys.

Continuity may be the central stream of memory. Time is not corpuscular, but a current. Memory is able to record the flow so that now and then are connected by more than coincidences of comparison and contrast. There is something whole we are a part of and memory extends the full length of life (or nearly the full length) to keep us aware of that gift.

All those Christmas presents linger with a certain ambivalence in my memory. When we were distributing the contents of the parental home after Mom's death, my siblings insisted a Noah's ark and a Lionel electric train were Christmas gifts to me "from Santa Claus." I have some memory of playing with the Noah's ark (another of my parents' creations) with my siblings, but no memory that it was "mine". I have no memory at all of the Lionel train, and therefore feel there must be some other explanation. My memory also holds a certain ambivalence about the things I do remember getting. I felt I was supposed to be a great deal more enthusiastic about gifts than I actually was.

I don't know to what degree I am imposing later values when I say this, but I think I felt a measure of increased responsibility in regard to each thing I received that seriously modified any straightforward exuberance over getting them.

I remember spending quite a bit of time each summer of my childhood with my Grandfather and Aunt Mimi. Aunt

Mimi, my Grandmother's sister, married my Grandfather after my Grandmother died. They always spent their summers in Montana, although they lived the rest of the year in Long Beach, then Laguna Beach, California. They drove a two-toned, orange and white Buick with the distinctive exhaust ports on the side. My Grandfather enjoyed driving around Chouteau County visiting acquaintances, some of whom were tenants on land he owned or used to own, and others who were political or farm organization friends.

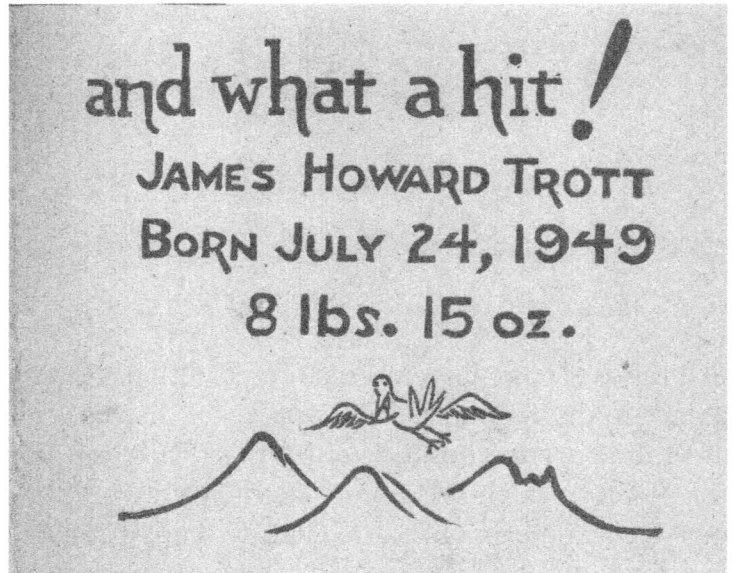

and what a hit!
JAMES HOWARD TROTT
BORN JULY 24, 1949
8 lbs. 15 oz.

Dad's handmade block print birth announcement.

I usually rode in the back seat where I could go to sleep when the bumpy roads had mesmerized me sufficiently. I remember few distinct events of these journeys, but I'd guess I spent hundreds of hours in that back seat.

Grandfather was a deep well of advice. He loved general apothegms that put forth principles to live by. "Early to bed, early to rise. . .," "A stitch in time saves nine," "A penny saved is a penny earned," and gems like, "One seldom regrets having eaten too little." I'm pretty sure this last was from a famous book very popular among the homesteading generation, by one Dr. Rasmus Larssen Alsaker. It was full of bold statements about how to restore and maintain one's health using common household items.

The Christmas star Dad put up on front of the house each year.

Grandfather's devotion to Alsaker reminded me of the O. Henry story "The Handbook of Hymen" which features two bachelor prospectors who spend the winter in a cabin with only two books which they tossed coins for. One of the books was Herkimer's *Handbook of Indispensable Information*, and the other was Kahlil Gibran's *Prophet*. The upshot was the next spring they both courted the same woman, applying all they'd learned that winter, which is to say, each constantly quoted his own book, to an equitable result you'll have to find yourself. The story is worth the read.

The "principled" approach to advice-giving was universal among my mother's family, the Hanfords. A properly serious and didactic tone was used and if all the principles and advice were recorded, it would fill an encyclopedia. I believe my wife and children would testify I often take this approach to instruction.

Photo for a Christmas card, 1960?

Larger family gatherings were common – regularly at Thanksgiving, 4th of July, etc. and frequent on birthdays, especially the summer ones. Mine was July 24th, so it often formed the basis for a camping trip with cousins, or a combined birthday (a couple of cousins had birthdays close by on the calendar) all-day picnic, barbeque, sports and general gabble at one of the five farms. Most frequently, perhaps, we gathered at Uncle Norris Hanford's or Uncle Burton Long's. Sometimes we'd all gather in the Highwood or Shonkin mountains, especially later when Robinsons bought an old cabin up there.

DAD OF MANY DIMENSIONS

Whenever the family gathered, my Dad added
considerably to the life of the party. He was beloved of all,
and always willing to be goofy or clever in ways
that entertained the cousins, but also the aunts and uncles.
However, for reasons no doubt accessible only to deep
psychotherapy, I often found my Father's popular goofiness
uncomfortable. I recall one greater family outing to Glacier
Park when we stopped to eat (at East Glacier I think) filling up
five or six tables with assorted cousins, aunts, etc., and Dad
had the whole place laughing uproariously at his hi-jinks.

Pete, Jimmy, and Andy on the scratchy old blue couch.

I did not enjoy it, however, but felt embarrassed or ashamed – a most peculiar reaction, and one I can't quite sort out to this day. One thing I came to understand later, however – both my father and mother were youngest in largish families, while I was the oldest. There was some sense in which I felt that role in relation to them, too!

Dad teaching me "Five Little Piggies Went To Market".

But that was only one of Dad's faces. I have a wide range of memories of my father, of whom I feel safe in saying he was easily the most important person in my life. My favorite memories of him are the dusty, smelly farmer (essences of sweat and diesel) who arrived home late at our house in town during the working months early spring to late fall. He almost always got home after the rest of us had finished supper and so he ate his alone. He wore a plain billed cap and black leather engineer boots, with a t-shirt and blue jeans during the warmer days, and seemed the very epitome of what a man ought to be. He always kept his sense of humor – so much so that the few times I remember him angry stand out very much. Each night he was tired and it was obviously a good tired – well-earned and to be emulated. He was gentle and still full of jokes.

Dad dressed up with me not quite so much.

He also had a cleaned up, church-going or (in the earlier days) going-out-with -Mom appearance I admired. He used a drop of Old Spice cologne in those occasions and I still love the fragrance. On Sundays he was in suit and tie, and looked

more at home in them than most of the farmers at church. He
wore his dressed up look also on occasions when he went out
canvassing for Farm Bureau or Chouteau County Republicans.
Handsome and respectable, but not quite the man he was in
his dirty farm duds. I didn't realize until much later, that his
father had worn a suit to work most of his working life.

From old 8mm movie, Dad's first year farming with Norris.

Although he was 29 when I was born, Dad was
remarkably youthful. He was lively and nimble as well as
strong and vigorous. It was hard to imagine any work that
would be too much for him. I remember very few times when
he ran up against physical limitation – one being the time a
faulty radiator cap on the combine ended up scalding him

pretty badly. But he lost no work over it, despite what must have been considerable pain for a few days.

Dad and Mom both loved the odd expression, and a true scholar could put together a considerable collection of "sayings" gathered over the years. Pete became a great Dickens fan, and added some fine examples from *Little Dorrit*. Mr. F.'s aunt, who became quite vociferous in her dotage (one must employ a strident voice) saying things like, "When we lived in Henley, Barnes's gander was stole by tinkers!" and "I hate a fool!" and "What he come then there for?" and (as she was led from the room) "You can't make a head and brains from a brass doorknob!"

Dad leading hi-jinks, family going "back-to-nature".

Once when my college friend, Steve "Zoe" Rennard, visited us at the farm with his new bride, he and she joined in our evening hi-jinks and game of tag with the kids as I drove the model T around behind the crowd. Zoe started chasing Barbara around the Quonset building calling out with his best Hollywood Indian accent, "Me chase-em white woman, ho, ho, ho!" This saying stuck and was used thereafter on occasions when an exuberant utterance seemed necessary and none other was immediately available.

Dad had quite a few of these odd expressions collected in childhood. None of us knows the origins of "American lackadodies with persnakdino sauce". Scottish expressions were often used, such as "'ee lacks a shingy," and "ee could no hit a barn door w' a banjo." Some of these undoubtedly came from Uncle Bob's Scottish in-laws. Dad had a number of sayings with ancient roots such as "Well, I'll be go to sea," which Matt thinks came from Grandfather Gus. This with other sayings originated with earlier generations in Maine. For instance a standard answer when someone asked "What are you doing?" was "Picking blueberries." At points of disagreement he had a mock-threat he'd commonly call up in an Irish accent, "How'd you like a nice poke in the gob?"

Mom's photo of Dad's photo of Malibu the antelope.

Grandfather Hanford had an expression that something very snug was "tighter than Dick's hatband." Looking it up years later in *Brewer's Dictionary of Phrase and Fable,* I was surprised to discover it went back to Richard Cromwell, Oliver's son, whose term as Lord Protector, as successor to his father, was short and unsuccessful. The saying was that the crown (or hat) did not fit him – "tighter than Dick's hatband". I had a sudden vision of fourteen generations of Hanfords repeating their fathers' saying, with twelve generations having no idea of its origins!

A number of Dad's expressions were tinged by what is sometimes called bathroom humor. One example occurred in a response to something stated that was unclear either in enunciation or content, "stepped in what?"

He picked up a few more from his Army Air Corps service during World War Two, such as "stuff that in your barracks bag," and "catch that and paint it blue.".

Another came from his Aunt Alice, whom the kids at 85 Central would always try to offer graham crackers when she visited. Their motive was getting her to make her invariable reply, "I can no eat graham crackers, they make me fat," only the last syllable, tinged by her (Scottish) accent, came across to them as "fahrt".

Childish sayings were treasured – like "I saw off," for "I fell off," and from my cousin Joy, whom Dad sometimes entertained when she was a toddler: "Gwine a reebus," meaning, "We're going to the [Shawsheen] river," was also of her coinage. My childhood friend Merlin Ulrich contributed "I goan bie you!"

Contemporary idiom sometimes struck Dad's funny bone as in the expression "freakin' far out!" which he used excessively one summer. I remember we were building a bin. Part of the operation involved four of us hoisting up a big pole for a block and tackle and setting it temporarily in a posthole. Just as we were all lifting and straining to get the thing in position Dad employed a high stage voice to holler, "freakin' far out!" and all of just about had hernias between lifting and laughing at the same time.

Going through some of Dad's papers, Matt found a short handwritten list headed "85 Central St. sayings." Apparently Grandfather Gus originated the penchant for the odd expression. The list includes "Goodness gracious Agnes, isn't the ocean dusty?" "Wake me early, Mother, for I'm to be Queen of the May." "Chase me, Charlie, I've got barley up the leg of my drawers." "You heard me, you ain't blind." Then two more for which context must have been important – "No. 7 building [Danvers]" and "What's about the wire."[4] The final entry on this list is "Susabella Kissproof Jones," a nickname Dad or his brothers gave one of their teachers.

One expression originated from an episode when Dad was in college. As a commuter, Dad had a more disjointed college career than the resident students. He lived in Andover and drove or rode to Boston, sometimes with various kinsmen (Uncle Walter and Uncle Bob) or rode the train. Along with the other non-resident students, he was a member of Dudley House. He did not make a lot of friends in college, but had a small group of fellows he was close to. They used to go to Chinese restaurants, and other activities together, including at least one concert. Dad couldn't recollect for sure, but he thought it was at Sanders Theater. The performers that night were four members of a string quartet. Dad's friends who went with him were Ted Kalem, Eliot Howes and one other.

Dad fully intended to enjoy the concert and went honestly and without malice with that intention. But from the first, there was something that struck him and his friends about it . The string quartet consisted of three tall fellows playing violin and cello. All of these looked serious-minded and even grim. But the fourth musician was a very short fellow, and he, of course, was playing the string bass. This tickled Dad's funny bone. The four Dudleyites controlled

---

[4] *Pete points out Dad explained this one in his own childhood memoir *Astray in Eden*, p. 33.

themselves fairly well, however, until Eliot Howes leaned over, and intoned in a bass voice of his own, "they <u>beat</u> him."

From then on each nuance contributed, and less and less control was exhibited, except for Howes, who was, according to Dad, exasperatingly able to remain calm while he caused everyone else to blow their gaskets. Halfway through the concert, an official came down the aisle from the back. He leaned over to the four undergrads and asked bitingly, "Why do you come!" This of course only contributed to the melee. Finally the foursome stumbled to their feet, and red-faced and sputtering walked up the long aisle and out into the cool Cambridge night. "They beat him," and "Why do you come!" were thus engraved in the collection of deathless sayings.

Dad was a lot of fun, but he could get very serious, and as I said, I do remember him getting mad a couple times. Once was in that same kitchen of the first memory. He had begun tickling me, and I wanted him to stop. I said so, at which point he just tickled harder and seemed almost angry at my protests. I think my whining bothered him. From what I've learned since, I think it was a complex situation which partly threw him back to the days when his brothers teased him unmercifully. Perhaps my complaining seemed to imply he was bullying me like they bullied him, and reminded him of the pain of being humiliated by them. One of my daughters used to hate me tickling her, and I had close to the same mixed reaction when she protested.

Another time I look back at with incredulous chagrin, as resulting from one of those unthinking things on my part which kids are so capable of. Cousin Marilyn was visiting us at the farm and sat to my left at supper, while Dad sat at the head of the table and I to his left. He had been working in the field all day, then showered and come to dinner barefoot. Marilyn realized this, leaned over and whispered to me, "Stomp on your dad's foot!" This I proceeded to do, quite firmly. As I imagine I would have done, he rose up and back-handed me. I believe that was pretty much the end of it, except I remain amazed I did as was suggested to me!

I think in general I was well "spoiled" along the Dr. Benjamin Spock lines, especially in the early years. As is often the case, I think my parents gradually developed a more balanced (more disciplined) approach with my subsequent siblings. But at one point in adulthood I mentioned to Dad how often I got spanked and he scoffed and said I hardly got spanked at all. Perhaps the few spankings I remember were the only ones! I recall him once more quite angry on one of those occasions, yet I don't remember it being a very hard spanking.

Through some pretty good teaching in our church over the years I have come to feel strongly that discipline should not be administered in the heat of anger – yet my errors with my children have been fully as many as my parents'.

I have mentioned that both my parents were the youngest in fairly large families. I have often thought how hard it must have been to become child-supervisors with hardly any child-supervisory experience at all. As I've said, I think they spoiled me for the first three or so years, and were frustrated by how high maintenance I could be. In my early years I had bad dreams that were quite dramatic, and I often got up and went seeking help. Especially after my brother Pete was born, I think the additional interruption of parental sleep got hard to take and eventually I was bluntly told to go back to bed and save the accounts of my dreams for morning. So the black knight who rode up from the basement through the hot air return vent, and the great balls and rollers that threatened to flatten me against the floor of my dreamscapes went on scaring me until I gradually accumulated enough survival statistics to fall back on.

Dad had a wonderful reading voice and he seemed to enjoy reading us stories. He would do different voices and dramatic effects. I loved to be read to. I think we went through most of Thornton Burgess and innumerable shorter children's books. Dad was himself an accomplished illustrator, and he preferred the books best illustrated. I recall *Johnny Crow's Garden* was a favorite, and the *Hollow Tree Snowed-In*

Book. I think it was after Andy was born that we began *Dr. Doolittle*. A sharp memory for me is the chapter where Dr. Doolittle is at sea in a ship with the push-me-pull-you and various other animals, and a pirate ship looms on the horizon in hot pursuit. I cried out and begged Dad to stop reading, in something very like genuine terror. I think he finally realized I was in earnest and did end the evening's reading, but I know we went on to finish it so perhaps only one day was enough to steel myself for the deadly encounter to come.

Mom read to us, too, and took us on walks and errands, and did all the innumerable things Moms do to keep their little sweethearts occupied. I'm not sure how good I was at keeping myself entertained, but I recall messing about while Mom did ironing in the little "Sun Room" Dad built her just off the kitchen. She listened to various radio programs as she ironed, including Christian broadcasts, and I remember regularly hearing "Love Lifted Me," with its dramatic presentation of a scenario in which someone was sinking under when the captain of the ship reached out and rescued him. It was quite a few years before I had any idea who the captain of the ship was or what that rescue meant. Yet looking back down the years I see a seed planted there, or at least a furrow begun.

The other half of my heritage is in New England – indeed far more than half, when one realizes only a couple generations earlier (on my Mom's side) the Bates were in Vermont and New Hampshire while the Gwinns were in western Pennsylvania, and the Hanfords in Connecticut. But all the Trotts and my Dad were very much born Yankees.

So one year, when I was five or six the parents decided on a pilgrimage back east to Andover, Massachusetts, my Dad's home town. I have foggy memories of going cross country and stopping off in various places – again supplemented by photographs I've since seen. In Andover my closest cousin in age was Bobby, who was several years older, and who had another cousin closer to his age living nearby, Georgy Woods. (Bobby died this year – the first of my eastern cousins to go.) Their mutual grandparents (Scots immigrants with marvelous accents) also lived nearby and they had an early TV with a screen 8 by 10 inches or so – my first exposure to this advanced and somewhat magical technology. I had seen movies and I suppose they lessened the miracle a little.

On that early trip back east to Andover some mysterious flurry of events transpired which included Pete and I spending a lot of time with aunts and uncles and Mom and Dad being rather scarce. At one point Pete and I were given some nice new toys (machine guns? swords and shields?) for no apparent reason – no birthdays, not Christmas. Many years later, when I was in college and visited my Uncles and Aunts in Andover I learned from Uncle Bob that my Mom had a miscarriage there, and Dad and Bob buried my little sibling's remains in a Band-Aid can in the woods behind Bob's house. It was a strange experience to reflect upon that news. I cherish the prospect of meeting that brother or sister in eternity, along with several grandchildren we had no chance to get to know in this world.

Also on that trip, I managed to get bitten by the Woods' dachshund. I had limited exposure to dogs up to that time, but one day when things were slow at the Bob Trott's, I wandered next door where I discovered the dachshund in the yard, also apparently without occupation. I squatted down and petted him, and somehow managed to insult him to the degree he snapped at me with sufficient intent to tear my cheek on the right side of my nose. I was outraged and ran hollering and fairly bloody back to Aunt Cleo *et al*, who took me for stitches – perhaps that was when the new toys appeared. It was generally suspected that I had mistreated the dog, which was not so, but rather quite the reverse. I carried the scar proudly for years, indeed it's still there amongst the various topographical features of my craggy crust.

I believe our Partridge cousins were living in a big house in those days, and that it had been some damaged by a serious hurricane not too long before our visit. I also believe we visited the Allan Trotts in Bethel, Connecticut. Little rises to the surface to corroborate it nor does the return trip register.

34

Dad was the only Yankee among the Montana uncles. I did not know how much of a Yankee he was until much later – similarly I didn't really know he had any kind of "accent," as obvious as it was to other Montana natives. (Forty years after he settled there new acquaintances were still occasionally asking, "You aren't from here, are you?")

Not only was Dad a Yankee, but he was the first of perhaps eight generations of American Trotts to be born outside Maine. (After our first three generations who appear to have resided in Dorchester, Massachusetts. We think "the other Thomas Trott of Dorchester," an illegitimate 3rd generation colonist may be our direct ancestor in the New World. Thomas Jr., his father, was officially found to be such in a Dorchester paternity suit. Thomas, Sr., his grandfather, immigrated about 1638.)

In any case during the following years (circa 1715-84) in the wild New England woods, during which there were Indian wars every ten years, Trotts grew more stoic and pessimistic. This was exacerbated by the fact they always seemed to join the losing side in major conflicts – for instance between the Gorges Administration (the original patentee of Maine and Nantucket) and the Massachusetts Bay officers – possibly together with the somewhat heretical (said the Massachusetts divines) Rev. Mr. Wheelwright. Then, in the Revolution, with the British who had fortified the area in which they had recently settled, the Castine peninsula on Penobscot Bay.

The earliest ancestors we can provide reasonably certain documentation for were John and Lydia Trott, who lived in Falmouth (now Portland) in the 1730s, then settled with other relatives on land in Castine in the 1760s. Thus after the Revolution, they fled to New Brunswick, Canada, with others of "the Penobscot Loyalists," where they attempted to start over during a very hard winter. The heads of two of those families died within the first few years.

Several other family members perished in Canada before most of the remnant returned to eastern Maine and started over yet once again. To what degree does a family develop a pattern of expectations over generations? It seems to me all this had something to do with our perspectives.

Dad was admired for his fortitude and sense of humor, but he did not have a very high view of the human race. He often said you could tell which was the wrong opinion or wrong way to go in any given circumstance, because that was the way most people were going. In studying Robert Frost later in college, I came to the generalization that 20th century New England ended up with a philosophy that was Calvinism without God. Since Dad was a professed Agnostic during my growing up years, I think I could thus fairly characterize him.

While Dad represented masculine values to his sons – at the same time he repudiated the popular masculine image – the Hollywood cowboy, the tough guy, the two-fisted embodiment of machismo. Being an insecure lad, I kept double-checking what men were supposed to look like by studying the other men around me. By the grace of God, I had a pretty good bunch of men to watch – in addition to my father, my uncles, my grandfather, various scout leaders, and later one football coach, in particular.

Dad and I as amateur archaeologists at old Ft. McKenzie.

36

SIBLINGS AND COUSINS

Pete was almost three years younger than I – allowing enough time for me to be thoroughly spoiled. They told me I tried to trade him for a kitten not too long after he was born. However, I think the true account is that John Ayers, a wry old farmer who lived opposite us and down the street made the offer to me – "How would you like to trade that new baby brother of yours for a nice kitten?" And I being a polite sort of person agreed to the proposition. I cannot remember any great chagrin when the offer was rescinded, in fact I'm quite sure Pete proved much more satisfactory than any kitten.

April 1943

Hanford family gathered before my time (last time before Howard was killed). (from back) Norris, Mom, G-mother, G-father, Howard, Florence, Jean, Marian, Ronald, and Nancy.

At 5 my cousin David Dyrland came to stay with us for awhile (9 months). Dave's mother, my Aunt Jean was a psychiatric nurse who developed paranoid schizophrenia about the time her youngest daughter, Janice, was born. Despite the sometimes severe hardships they underwent, Jean's four children grew up to be respected and admired by all, and were special favorites among our cousins.

Trotts, Longs, GF & GM, Dyrlands and Hanfords

Dave and I attended kindergarten at Mrs. Mackenstadt's house. There we learned to finger-paint and made various small projects, some of which still decorated 1904 Franklin when my mother died. Among our classmates at Mrs. Mackenstadt's were Tommy Leinart, Rusty Peres, Clarice Holm, Jimmy Herbold, Rocky Tope, Theresa Morse, Jimmy Berg, and others. It was not a dramatic period for me, although Dave reminds me of a couple of his memories from the time. Our parents took turns car-pooling us to "school" and back. One day Tommy, who kept current on the movies, gangsters, etc., as he was delivered to his house, slammed the car door with a flourish and speaking to my father said ,"So long, Thucker!" with a boyhood lisp plus a Brooklyn accent.

My father added this to his collection of unique verbal flourishes hauled it out every now and then over the ensuing years. (My memory has a query footnoting this one – and sure enough my brothers aver the Leinart responsible for this famous saying was rather Tom's little brother, Billy.)

Grandmother with various cousins: Dave and me the babies.

One of the clearest memories I have about Dave's time with us is that on one of the many occasions when his Dad, Uncle Cliff, stopped by to see his son (which he often did as he commuted between his farm in Highwood and his farmland in Big Sandy) he brought a little toy car for Dave. And in the self-centered and selfish way that was natural to me, at the first opportunity I appropriated it, more or less snatching it out from under Dave's nose. At that point Uncle Cliff intervened, "Take it easy, young fella. You know he has feelings, too!" It sounds strange to say it, even now, but the thought that Dave –indeed that anybody else, had feelings, too, was entirely new to me – and it cut to my heart. Perhaps this was the first occasion on which my conscience was touched with genuine sympathy — or repentance.

Grandfather and his second wife, Aunt Mimi.

Such occasions must have been fairly uncommon. I remember quite a few times I was "caught" doing something I shouldn't have done, but generally all I regretted was being caught. However I remember another early lesson – possibly as early as 1956 or so, when I took ten cents out of my mother's purse without asking, and went down with Tommy Leinart to buy some candy at the Pioneer Mercantile store. When we got back, Mom was entertaining Aunt Mimi, and when they asked who had given us the candy, Tommy and I spoke up at once – with different stories. He loudly denied the idea that he had bought the candy, so I was left holding the bag. After I confessed, Aunt Mimi took me aside, sat me on her lap, looked into my eyes, and said, "I'm very disappointed in you, Jimmy." That one went more deeply than any discipline.

Tommy Leinart with a captured bird.

As a kindergartner I recall being for a while overwhelmed with the blueness of blue. It seemed more than a color – a presence or an atmosphere so full as to color not only mind and mood, but even sight and smell. Everything had a tinge of blue, looked blue, smelled blue. The whole world for a time did homage to blue.

Drew (known as Andy in his youth) was born in February, while I was still in kindergarten. I don't really remember Pete's advent, but Drew's I do. He was born with strabismus and we were fascinated with his unique talent to operate his eyes independently. From pretty early on he was made to wear a patch over the "non-lazy" eye. We were not satisfied until after a great deal of practice, we, too, could look cross-eyed with one eye.

But Drew went through quite a bit of medical "practice" – patches, surgeries, and glasses from a very early age. He

41

was nonetheless or partly because of this, quite bold and brave from early on. Putting up with the pain of medical procedures may have had something to do with that. He was not only irresistibly "cute," but he had a lively intellect and sense of humor that made him universally beloved. I think it is accurate to say we imitated these characteristics, but not to any degree of success. By the age of five Drew could pretty much identify any make and model of car, and wax eloquent on a wide range of subjects. He was a particular favorite of cousin Howard Dyrland, who enjoyed long conversations with him.

Proud older brother holding the early Drew.

"Grandfather" to us and "Father" to his children, J. Arthur Hanford, was distinctly the Patriarch to most of us – at least into our middle teens. He was born in Chicago where his hard-working father, Edwin Henry Hanford, ran a store. They

were poor and thrifty. Edwin would bring coal home in a
gunny sack. The boys collected the gunny sacks which were
redeemable for a nickel each, as well as tin cans (a nickel), beer
bottles (a nickel), lard pails (not too rusty, a dime) and
whiskey bottles (a dime). He once told us when he found a
whiskey bottle he would take it to the local saloon. There
while remaining strictly outside the evil establishment, he
would climb up on the hitching rack and wave the empty
above the swinging doors until the proprietor saw him and
came out to exchange it for his dime.

Robinson, Dyrland & Trott cousins with & at the Longs, ca 1957.

Edwin Henry continued to run the store until he had
accumulated enough capital plus a pledge of support from a
childless relative, on the strength of which he moved to

Oakesdale, Washington and eventually set up several lines of business, chiefest of them being an orchard, and a bank. The legacy of the orchard was grandfather knew a lot about fruit.

The legacy of his father's hard work and business acumen showed up in most of his children, although in various ways. A couple of them started car dealerships, and expanded the banking business. Others set out homesteading. In fact for a short while, several of them were in something of a homesteading partnership on the Camas Prairie in Idaho.

Grandfather, J. Arthur Hanford, in 1911.

Edwin Henry believed in doing things thoroughly, so when he decided to build a home in Oakesdale, he found an eminent hill, and there he built what is still known as "The Castle," or "The Hanford Castle." There are similar homes in the older wealthier sections of Philadelphia, but very few as grand in the west!

Grandfather was brought up to high moral standards that included no consumption of alcohol and no use of tobacco. Except for the trade in beer and whiskey bottles back in Chicago, he adhered strictly to these rules.

Howard D., Ron & Dave, Nancy & me, Howard H., Marilyn, 1949.

After the move to Oakesdale Grandfather once stopped by a new brick house up on the hill, which became known as the Fish place. The carpenters and masons were at work on this building, and one of them had left a big quid of tobacco lying on a saw horse. His mother, Carrie Metella Brooks Hanford, had always exhorted Arthur against the evils of tobacco, so Grandfather picked up the slab of the evil stuff and hightailed home. When he got there, he presented it to his mother saying, "Mother, you said that it was wrong to use tobacco, so I took this away from the carpenters up at the Fish place." Whereupon she, with peculiarly mixed feelings replied, "Arthur, you're right, it is wrong to use tobacco, and I hope you never will, but that tobacco belongs to those men

45

and to take it is stealing. They have a right to use it if they want, since they bought it with their own money." Then she sent him back. He went with fear and trembling and quickly deposited it back on the sawhorse where evidently it hadn't been missed, then ran for home faster than the first time.

One time in Oakesdale, Grandfather and Percy and John got ahold of a piece of porous rattan buggy-whip, which they took out in the fresh-plowed orchard in order to smoke it, as was the fashion among boys. However their father happened by, and he said to them, "I see you boys mean to smoke. This is a good opportunity for me to tell you what I think about it. I think it's a low habit that's bad for your health and your pocketbook and I'd like you boys to promise me you'll never use tobacco." So they all promised and Grandfather was proud to say none of them ever did use tobacco. The legacy continued in the next generation, although I think both Howard and Norris smoked while they were in the Navy. But one summer when I worked on the Long farm, Aunt Marian recited to me a moral apothegm, no doubt of Hanford origins, "A man who uses tobacco will use alcohol, and a man who uses alcohol will do anything!" Since my father smoked a pipe, I felt slightly offended by the implications. Since I chewed tobacco for a while, I suppose I qualified, too.

Although I only became cognizant of the fact later in life, perhaps because his moral emphases were compatible with a similar emphasis in the Methodist circles I was familiar with, grandfather's religious heritage was actually Unitarian Universalist. He told us that back in Chicago he and his brothers were supposed to accompany their sister Bertha to Sunday School, but they got to where they generally played hooky, instead.

Grandfather remembered once when he was about five, he stayed out on the boulevard instead of going in to Sunday School. It was a cold day and pretty soon his nose began to run. Then a gentleman from their same church stopped on his way in and said to grandfather, "Say, buddy, I'll give you a

46

penny if you'll let me wipe your nose." So he did those two
kindnesses, but when he got to church he told on grandfather,
and grandfather ended up spending the rest of the day in bed
for discipline.

Coin and Yuki Sekiya, who worked for the Edwin Hanfords.

Grandfather grew up with dogs and he often told
stories about them. When they were young his brother Roy
had a big mastiff named Coin. Coin chased rabbits and he did
it doggedly, so to speak. Once Grandfather and Percy and
John were out in the orchard where they were supposed to
burn a large pile of branches pruned from their father's apple

trees. The pile was big because it was the entire season's accumulation, and had gradually become a haven for many rodents. After they lit the pile a cottontail rabbit realized something was amiss and came charging out of the pile, much to Coin's delight. The dog took off on what was to prove very hot pursuit indeed.

The pile of dried branches burned very quickly and within a short time its center was a heap of livid coals, too hot to get anywhere near. Meanwhile Coin and the cottontail had run their leg in the old dog and rabbit race. The rabbit was getting tired, since cottontails are more dodgers than runners, and its instinct was to go back to the place it had long found refuge. Apparently the panting mastiff right behind it had driven away the recent recollection that something was not quite right at home. So the rabbit came dashing back right into the base of the fire, and grandfather says they could see it crumple and die before their very eyes.

Coin, however, was "hot" on the rabbit's tail, and it was not until he had dashed into the fire himself, and snatched up the dead rabbit, that his sense returned and he dropped it again, and left the inferno as quickly as he'd come. The dog coughed a lot for the next few weeks, but otherwise seemed none the worse for wear. Even his feet which had travelled over some very warm ground, seemed to be all right.

Also as a boy in Oakesdale Grandfather had a Llewelyn setter named Shot. One early spring day the boys all walked down the railroad track next to the lake where all during the winter ice had been cut. The icemen would take their saws and chisels and sleds down and cut great blocks which they hauled back and packed in sawdust in an ice house, and thereafter they would sell these in smaller chunks for summer refrigeration.

Shot was a retriever and delighted in water as most good retrievers do. Without giving adequate thought to the outcome, the boys threw a stick in the open water where the ice had been cut. The dog leaped in and retrieved it, then swam back to the edge. However, the edge of the pool was vertical ice, perhaps a foot high, and the dog could not get any purchase on it in order to get out. He tried again and again. The boys were pretty young and were afraid to go out in the ice too near him, nor could they think of any other ways to extricate the dog from the freezing water. They had often been warned to stay away from the ice, and now they had a dilemma. Although Shot kept trying to lunge up and climb out, he fell back each time.

The boys were increasingly sure each attempt would be his last. Finally Grandfather had an idea. He told the others their only hope was to run away from the lake as though they were abandoning the dog. This they did and a hundred yards away they looked back and there came the dog lickety-split. Grandfather said he had never felt more relief in his life, and never appreciated a dog more. They never knew just how the dog escaped. I believe Grandfather ended the tale with the customary moral. The story might be taken to show that kindness is not always kindness and doing something hard-hearted is occasionally the most merciful thing.

At some point the Oakesdale Hanfords began to go to Priest Lake in northern Idaho for family vacations. Some third and fourth generation cousins still go there to this day. There are many stories of the idyllic place, but Grandfather told one that furnished a by-word throughout the family.

It seems that Grandfather and Uncle Homer went there one summer with a lady chaperone and a couple of younger ladies. The pines were green and the lake was cool. One morning Grandfather got up early and decided to take a dip on his own. Wild country that it was, and being alone as he was, Grandfather decided to swim au naturel. He left his clothes in a pile and waded in, then swam around for a while, when turning toward the shore, he saw one of the girls who had come with Uncle Homer sitting on a log and watching him. She, too, seemed to be enjoying the morning and gave no evidence of any plans to leave. Grandfather was getting cold, but still the girl sat there.

Grandfather & Grandmother & Marian, Camas Prairie 1915.

Never being one to bow to pressure, Grandfather decided to out-bluff her. He turned and deliberately began to wade out of the water toward shore and his audience. It wasn't long before she rose abruptly and departed toward camp. That morning at breakfast, trying once more to make him uncomfortable, the girl piped up and announced, "I know a funny story on Arthur," to which, without blinking, he replied, "YOU tell." And "YOU tell," became an expression used as challenge and counterpoint on other awkward occasions.

Grandfather and his sister and several brothers homesteaded on Camas Prairie, Idaho. There he met my

Grandmother, Louise Gwinn, and there they lived after they were married. My oldest aunt, Marian, was born in their fancy homestead shack. Although the evidence is scanty, it appears grandfather and my grandmother had serious disagreements about religion while they were courting, she being raised as a Cumberland Presbyterian. In fact her father, David Howard Gwinn was from several generations of Presbyterians, and was for a while partner with the Cumberland Presbyterian minister on the *Garfield Enterprise* newspaper.

The homestead years extended from the Camas Prairie to Shonkin and Highwood, Montana, but those years are recounted more thoroughly than I can do it in a few other places, so I will not repeat the few details I know. One account of the Camas Prairie venture, a fictionalized version, may be found in *The Gods of Soldier Mountain* by Aunt Katherine Hanford, Great-uncle Roy's wife. It's far from good history, but has its own peculiar perspectives. My Mom and Dad collected Arthur and Louise's letters in a thick volume which was privately printed in 20 or so copies, entitled *Hanford-Gwinn Letters: 1912-1951.*

The only one of my Grandfather Hanford's siblings I knew at all was Uncle Percy, although I met Uncle John once or twice. Uncle Percy was the Bachelor of the family.

Besides being the only unmarried one among his siblings, he was also the only radical. For a time he attended a school of economics in Chicago, but from the hearsay I picked up either it was a different institution than the famous Chicago School of Economics, or he disagreed strongly with what he learned there. Percy presented Dad with an elaborate plan for turning our Shonkin farm into a commune. I have a copy of his "Corporate Rural Livelihood: a Plan for Cooperative Farming." Although American history has a number of instances where this idea was tried, I think Percy was one of the few people advocating it in the 50's. Dad demurred at the suggestion we participate.

Uncle Percy would come around almost every summer in our early days. He drove one of those big solid-cab Willy's

Jeeps, and he timed his trips peculiarly to coincide with things like huckleberry season in the mountains. I remember Uncle Percy elaborating on his berry-picking methods about which he had not only given long thought, but much practice. He had built his own "rakes" which were sort of like big dust pans with long dowel fingers attached to the bottom lip and spaced just right to rake out the berries from among the smaller twigs and leaves.

Marian, Howard, Norris, Jean & Florence, at Shonkin, 1923.

I also recall his technique for separating the berries from the inevitable leaves and twigs by means of a wool blanket stretched at just the right angle. The berries would roll to the bottom, but the wool would catch and hold back the less mobile leaves and twigs.

Dad liked to repeat one of Uncle Percy's sayings. He didn't particularly like children, and he referred to them as "sticky flies and little green worms."

As the older one, Dave deserved more respect than I gave him.

The rest of the family didn't fully approve of Uncle Percy. My strongest memory of him was the time we visited Oakesdale when I was twelve or so, and he gave me a pair of handmade work boots. He had made these himself from scratch, using the finest black harness leather, well-saturated with neats-foot oil, and he instructed me about taking care of them. I destroyed them in about two months. I look back in horror at the way I waded through mud and water, with never a moment given to maintaining them in their original magnificent condition. I think if I had taken care of them I could still be wearing them today! Kids have little sense!

Gazing over Ft. Benton from the high bluffs across the river.

Photo Mom and Dad used on the Christmas card in 1956

LIFE IN TOWN

Fort Benton, the little town I grew up in, had various claims to fame, which some of the more satirical of my high school classmates turned into acronyms. It was the oldest continuous settlement in Montana (OCS), so it was known as "The Birthplace of Montana" (BOM). During its heyday in the Montana gold rush of the 1860's it grew to a size where some called it "The Chicago of the Plains" (COP). It was the county seat of Chouteau county (CSCC), and because it was the last port of navigation (LPON) on the Missouri River during steamboat days, it was also known as the farthest inland water port of the world (FIWPW). All this despite a permanent population of no more than 1900 in my youth and fewer now! The remains of the old American Fur Company fort and post were a source of pride, and the town has gradually accumulated no less than three museums and quite a few more historic sites. For all of that, it was just one more of hundreds of small towns in Montana.

It is easy to idealize one's experience, more so the farther one travels in time from the experience itself. But I think small town life in Montana after World War Two had some precious elements that have since faded.

The concept of "community" is one all peoples in all places recognize but only achieve to limited degrees. As a child in Fort Benton I was very much part of a community including but apart from my immediate and wider family connections. No child could go wandering off without someone intervening. No youngster could utter bad language or act disrespectfully toward anyone in authority without repercussions. There was a fairly extensive agreement on "community standards," and these were not essentially hateful or prejudiced against any group of persons, so long as no one transgressed basic decency in his public behavior.

A wide latitude of personalities and peculiarities were accepted without question or pressure to conform. Political and religious affiliations across the spectrum were recognized with no sense that any should be forbidden or penalized. Part of the community understanding had to do with remaining congenial and courteous despite disagreement. The idea of publically venting rage was unheard of, except perhaps in slurred accents on a late Friday or Saturday night in front of the bars along the river.

There were no dangerous people or places (discounting common physical or natural dangers.) There were no unapproachable aristocrats. There were no untouchable *hoi-poloi*.

But, of course, I am idealizing to some extent, and I was blissfully ignorant to some of what went on. Nonetheless I would extend my argument this far – to cite some evidence of real community life.

All the organizations in town could expect some sort of community support for their activities. If the Odd Fellows had a picnic, or the Mormons or the Jaycees had a booth at the fair, if the Methodists had an anniversary dinner or the athletic association sponsored a dance – a large part of the community would turn out in support.

The county fair was attended by one and all. Once or twice a year, community plays and musicals were put on with wide participation. Junior high and high school dances were sponsored by various classes and a junior and senior prom took place every year. Band and chorus concerts as well as several high school plays filled the large junior high auditorium. And every athletic event was packed with both home fans and "visiting" team supporters. It was nothing for football fans to drive 60 miles to a game, and buses from the high school took the pep band and others. Basketball tournaments brought out a considerable percentage of every community involved, often for several days.

"Who threw this bottle!"

Dad was conscripted for the part of a Cockney policeman in a community play during his early days in town. His principle line was "Who threw this bottle!" which he practiced assiduously in the basement.

There is little point in bemoaning what is no more, but it seems to me that the idea that we are first citizens of the world, second of America, third of Montana and only then of our little communities, stands things on their heads. Families and little communities are where real relationships and community life happens. The rest falls in to place where these are held sacred. The great question for succeeding generations is "Where does my community lie?" TV, media and the internet have made this question increasingly more difficult to answer, especially for city dwellers.

There was a baseball/softball stadium at our end of town where local leagues played in my earliest days, but it was demolished and the leagues faded.

In Fort Benton in those days, in addition to all the community forms of entertainment, "the movies" were shown every weekend at the Capital Theatre on Front Street across from the Missouri River, an enterprise owned and managed by the Arnst family. Again vague memories rise up (my father used to refer to his memory in borrowed terms – where from? George Burns? – as being like rice pudding with raisins floating to the top). I recall my Mother taking me to see movies that I didn't understand but nonetheless mildly enjoyed. Later the Arnsts moved with the times and built a drive-in theatre in the northwest corner of the town. It remained a favorite place of weekend recreation up through high school. Indeed I once took my friend Rachel Vielleux to the drive-in in my Ford model T truck!.

Our home had lots of music. The parents bought a nice stereo in a pair of cabinets, which often filled the living room where they sat with classical pieces or songs from the musicals. We kids had an older record player in our front bedroom, and there we listened to cowboy, folk, and variety tunes, memorizing quite a lot of music effortlessly. Mom and Dad would occasionally break into duets featuring the more poignant (still to me the most beautiful) songs like "Moon River," " Danny Boy," " Sentimental Journey," "Shenandoah," "Loch Lomond," "Auld Lang Syne " and so on.

I have an early memory of Mom taking me to the "other" drug store in Fort Benton on the corner where my nieces now run the Wake-Up Coffee House in the old Culbertson building across from the old bridge. There were a series of booths with juke-box controls in each, and Mom put in a quarter and played "How Much is the Doggy in the Window" (female artist) – the first clear recollection of pop music I have, although, as I've said, my mother did listen to the radio at home – and I must have heard pop tunes there.

Speaking of drug stores, I don't think it was until I was in junior high school that a classmate told me the story of when our fathers first met. This must have occurred when we were living in the Mary Katzenberger house on Front Street – most of the first year of my life. Someone in our family had a prescription, which was called in to what we used to call "Larson's Pharmacy" (later Benton Drug Store.) Dad went to pick up the drugs. The pharmacist on duty was Irving Nottingham, father of my classmate, Raedene. Dad walked up to the pharmacist's window and inquired, "Do you have something for the Trotts?" Mr. Nottingham didn't blink an eye, but gesturing across the aisle, replied, "There's a whole shelf full right over there."

Our home in Fort Benton at 1904 Franklin Street.

Our name was very susceptible to a host of puns, and mispronunciations ("Trout" is what a lot of people seemed to hear us saying) and we heard them all. In high school football the coach referred to me as "Trotsky".

Before the Katzenberger house we lived in an apartment in the Hagen Block –and sometime around 1952 we moved into 1904 Franklin Street, where most of my memories were formed. Grandfather and Grandmother had lived there from the late 1940s, moving there from the Robinson farm.

I started first grade in 1955. I recall Mom sitting me down at the dining room table and trying to teach me to write my name. I could not get the "J" right way around, and ended up frustrated to tears. Although I did not learn the word until I was in college, I was dyslexic. How thankful I am no one stuck that label on me then. I had to learn my way around it and do what everybody else had to do – rather than having all expectations lowered to fit my disability.

First grade & Mrs. Jo Sorkness, my teacher & later friend.

It manifests itself now, for instance, in typing "itself" at the beginning of this sentence. It seems I do right hand – left hand transpositions more and more as I grow older. I also have found throughout my life that where I have to distinguish between two things or people, I am about 75 percent sure to err, while more complicated distinctions are much easier for me. We had six or seven sets of twins in our church here in Philadelphia over the years, and I never got any of their names sorted out!

First grade was a bit of a speed bump, although kindergarten paved the way. Dave had moved back home and started school in the even smaller town of Highwood. The baby boom was in full swing with three first grades in Fort Benton in those days. So backward "J" or not, off I went where I had a patient and attentive teacher in Mrs. Jo Sorkness. She tailored her teaching to individual students, and we all learned our letters, phonics and the joy of reading.

I found Laurie's advent welcome despite my expression here.

Mrs. Sorkness' sons were to become best friends of my brothers, Andy and Jon, later on. Her youngest son, Tom, who lives in Philadelphia, has been my friend for a number of years. His mother also moved to Philadelphia, and I had the privilege of consulting with my first grade teacher up until recently, when she, too, parted company with us.

Laurie came along a couple years after Andy. A girl was a great novelty by that time and a joy to all. After she could walk, she and Andy were to become the Bobbsey Twins, doing a great deal together, and most often seen in tandem.

One of my first opportunities to doubt my memory occurred six years later at a Junior High dance held in the cafeteria just down the hall from that first grade classroom. I mentioned an incident I "remembered" from first grade when I had turned around to talk with a girl, and got myself banished to the hall. When I mentioned the "recollection" to the girl (with whom I was dancing), she told me she wasn't even in that class! Self-doubt is a gift, but not easy to receive.

My second grade teacher on that same hallway was Mrs. Hough who became my piano teacher of six years. The poor lady needed patience, especially in the piano lessons.

Jonathan came along about two years after Laurie. He had red hair which soon became apparent. In his early days he was in his own world. No doubt these days we all would have some label or other attached. Like Andy Jon was born with strabismus and underwent surgery, with the result he has no "fusion center," another visual technicality which we learned all about.

Christmas card photo circa1957, including Jonathan.

Jon's eyes were apparently sending independent non-fused images to his brain. He says he quickly learned to ignore one "picture" or the other. Jon didn't talk until he was four, and just about the time the parents were really getting worried, he began to speak at some length

My third grade teacher was Miss Langowski, whom I remember as pretty motherly, but cannot give many other details about. I remember the classroom was in the other hallway of the elementary school.

Pete and I ready for first day of school, 1958.

I had forgotten the name of my fourth grade teacher, Miss Hellig, until last year, when attending her husband's 60th High School reunion, she came over to visit with those of our class, who were also celebrating -- our 50th -- in Fort Benton. Joe Svoboda and Evie now live in Maryland not too far from our oldest daughter and family.

Matt was born in January when I was 9 ½. Another red head, he always had a unique sense of humor. Among other things, Matt and Jon represented Mom and Dad's efforts to balance out the gender disparity, but they ended up with five sons and only one daughter.

The family after Matthew came on the scene – me on camera.

I think I learned more from my siblings than they from me. I was often consciously imitating them, borrowing from their vocabularies and styles. I was often amazed at how much they knew (Pete and Andy knew most of the WWII airplanes, for example; and later, while I was stuck in the "folk era," all my siblings kept up with the times, delving into the rock scene).

Dad and Mom did several rounds of remodeling on our house at 1904 Franklin Street in Fort Benton. The first round involved removing the plaster and twin bookcases from the living/dining room so that it became one big room, with plasterboard and sliding Japanese screens (after 1974 when they visited us in Japan) inside the windows and some fancy indirect lighting and a coat closet just inside the front door. Also wall-to-wall carpet and wood paneling. I think I was seven or eight when that happened. I recall they hired our neighbor Don Scott, father of a classmate and friend, and his brother-in-law, George Baldwin.

Then not too many years later, perhaps about the time Laurie or Jon was born, Dad finished the second floor attic into two bedrooms, an office, and a bathroom leaving considerable storage space and a hallway beside the middle bedroom. Pete and Andy had the bedroom at the front of the house, I had the middle one, and as I said there was a hallway past my room with attic storage back in the eaves. That hallway, however, according to my brothers was occupied by two ghostly creatures by the names of White Eyes and Black Head.

The hallway had a light, but as I recall, it could only be turned on from the stairway end. In any case there was a period of time during which Pete and Andy swore to have been terrorized by these evil spirits, and for reasons I can't quite fathom to this day, my parents told me I would have to let them go through my room when they wanted to! My room had two doors, and I liked to keep them shut. I wanted it to be MY ROOM not a passageway for hagridden younger siblings. I found it intolerable that these "brats" had managed to persuade Mom and Dad in the matter.

At the peak of this conflict and my indignation, I made desperate plans. I hauled out a small slingshot I had won at some fair of the period, and when Andy came through the door on his merry way I let him have it nearly point blank with a stone, I suppose. He ran screaming down to the parents and I hightailed into the front bedroom where I tossed the criminal weapon out the window and into the flower patch near the front porch entrance. I then lied like a trooper, saying I had indeed thrown a rock at him – but only by hand! I do not recall the discipline I received.

I know that around that time and for a couple of years my parents became exceedingly skeptical of my veracity on many occasions. It got to where even if my brothers lied about an event, I was the one who was doubted. I had made my bed and had to lie in it! When I was eleven, recognizing this was a guaranteed path to failure, I resolved to change it. I distinctly recall talking to my Mother about this as she did laundry in the basement and telling her that I was going to tell the truth from then on. And for the most part, I did.

The hall battle subsided. I don't know what the final compromise looked like, but perhaps the ghosts faded or my territorial selfishness diminished.   That hallway was lined under the eaves with trunks – most of which came from my mother's Aunt Bertha who saved a huge quantity of valuable items, many of which we finally had to dispose of after Mom died. Also there was a wonderful hand-crank Victrola, which Dad would sometimes use to wake us on cold school mornings, playing "Mockingbird Hill" or "Ebbtide". It quite warmed our hearts, and no doubt began my affection for Victrolas since, several of which I have repaired.

Along with the regrettable tale of shooting my brother Andy with a slingshot, I should mention the time I shoved Pete's head through one of the glass bookcase doors in the living room/dining room. Strictly speaking, these twin bookcases, one on either side of the room, served as part of the constriction or partition that officially divided the two rooms and were eliminated in the renovations a few years later.

I do not know any more details of the event than that I was responsible for propelling Pete's head against the glass with enough force to break it (the glass, not his head, I don't think.). It was often mentioned, and almost always in those terms – "Jimmy shoved Pete's head through the glass door of the bookcase." This was repeated with the other, possibly abundant, evidence which established my reputation as prone to violence. I am happy to say, however, that I never tortured any kittens!

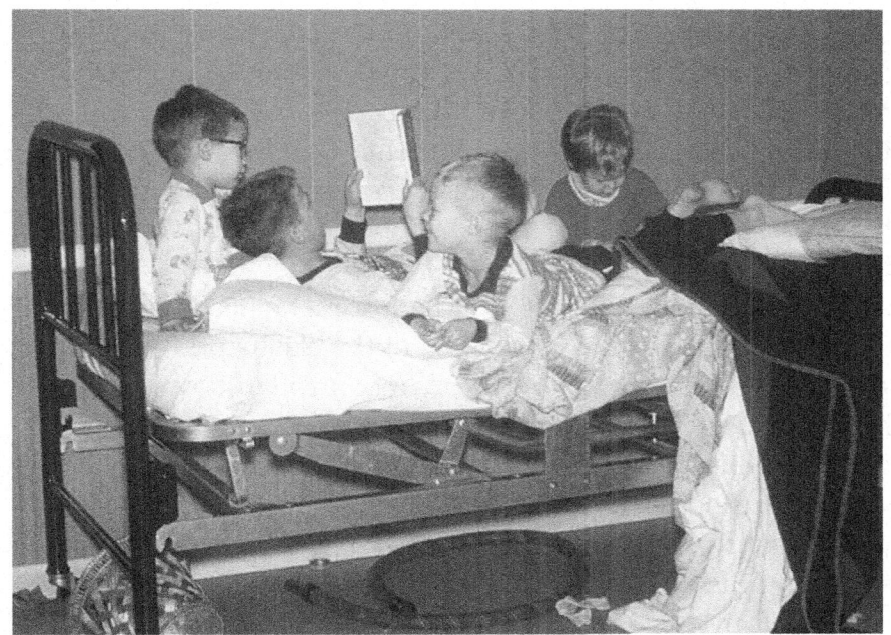

My bedroom apparently during a period of peace.

All my instincts are to come up with explanations which lessen the starkness of that description. But since I recall little, I cannot defend myself. Certainly there was violence in my soul. Pete and Drew saw much of the worst of it, with a few cousins and a few neighborhood friends coming in for their shares. I do not like to emphasize it, but it was a fact. I used physical force quite frequently when I felt it might be effective. Like other bullies, I much preferred to use it on persons smaller than myself. I was deeply impressed at my brothers' ability to resist my bullying on various occasions.

In particular I remember my admiration for Andy's resistance once time at the farm when I was sitting on his chest punching him and demanding that he do something or other or quit doing something or other, I'm not sure which. At any rate he simply refused – saying in effect, you may torture me, you may kill me, but you will not subdue me. This to me was extreme bravery and far beyond my own.

Pete and Andy occupied the front bedroom until I went to college, then Pete got a first floor bedroom to himself while Drew took over mine, and Matt and Jon moved up into the front bedroom. Laurie took over the first floor front bedroom next the living room. It was in that bedroom that Dad caught Jon and Matt at an infamous moment. Dad heard a strange noise, or rather sequence of noises, coming from the front of the house. He heard the same sounds again, and went to investigate.

When he got to the front bedroom, he heard the series of sounds, again, which consisted of the clash and tinkle of something breaking, followed by uncontrolled boyish laughter. He waited for the next series to be sure, and then realized what he was hearing, at which point he quickly opened the closet door, reached in and banged my two youngest brothers' heads together. They had just finished smashing the last of their sister's china doll dishes, inherited from their mother!

Once a week a lady named Mrs. Stoner came and helped Mom with house-cleaning. In retrospect I wonder if Grandfather financed this service – since I'm quite sure Mom and Dad had little in the way of funds before the mid-60s. In any case she was a regular feature of our lives and pretty much a member of the family. Photos indicate we older kids and our relatives attended her wedding sometime in the 50s. I know she worked for several other families around town, because she tended to report on the dramatic features of their households. I tremble to think what she had to say about us!

She was in many ways a warm and wonderful old soul, but she was among several rather outspoken racists I knew growing up. In retrospect I'm almost certain she had some

African genes, herself, and perhaps her harsh words about Black people were part of her tactics for "passing".

Mrs. Stoner with Matt in her lap at a family birthday party.

My "best friend" in Fort Benton during my younger years, perhaps until I was 12 or so was Bobby Culbertson, who now lives in California, (and whose wife is my Facebook friend). We spent countless hours with games and "wars" around the neighborhood, up in the hills, and down at the town dump, a favorite resort where treasures were sometimes found. As I reflect, I'm not sure what "best friend" means. It seems to have been a tradition that you were supposed to have a best friend, like Huck and Tom or Penrod and Sam, but Bobby and I had a certain temperamental compatibility that made us "best friends" despite having other good friends.

Conflict seems to have been an essential part of friendships in those dim and ancient days. One time I (a year older) "beat up" Bobby, which meant no more then than overcoming him and probably sitting on his belly while demanding he "give up". In any case his older sister Patty came upon her brother and his persecutor and immediately took action, snatching up a garden rake (steel-tined) and pursuing me down the sidewalk, lashing out with perfect timing to leave a set of punctures across my back. This of course cemented our friendship. (Mine and Bobby's – not mine and Patty's!)

On a later occasion just after he moved in across the street, Donny Scott and I introduced ourselves by throwing rocks at each other until we'd done some damage – and we too became fast friends.

Bobby Culbertson, one of my first best friends.

I received another set of punctures in connection with the Culbertsons. One time Bobby and I decided to take time out from our activities, seeking repose on a pile of old boards RJ (Bobby's dad) had piled against the back of the house. One of them sported a rusty nail which I had the good fortune to alight upon. I hurried home and reported my injury. However I did not receive the kind of sympathy such a serious wound deserved, and when one of the local doctors was called in (they often made house calls in those ancient times) Dr. Anderson added insult to injury by puncturing the other side of my posterior! Penicillin was the wonder drug which cured all our ills in those days.

One of my worst episodes with Bobby was the time we went up to a gravel pit between the dump and "the elevators" (the prairie version of the skyscraper – tall buildings along the railroad at the north end of town where grain was stored for loading in boxcars). I think it was Tommy Leinart, Bobby, his cousin Franky, and me, four of us on three bicycles. We looked through the gravel for "pretty rocks" and each had a pocketful or two when we decided to try riding the bicycles down the steep road back to the river bottom which the town is built upon.

I don't recall what order we went in, but Bobby and Franky went down together on one bike, and at the bottom, Franky flew off and landed on a pocketful of rocks. Although we tried to convince him that he was all right, he in fact had broken his leg. And senseless idiots that we were, Tom and I took off and went home to supper, without informing any adults of the plight of the two we left behind! Bobby eventually had to ride home leaving Franky behind, in order to tell his parents. I recall RJ coming over to our place and more in consternation than anger, asking why in the world I hadn't come and told someone. Perhaps mostly out of fear of being blamed, I hadn't even considered it!

I thought I remembered the details of that event contact with Bobby – pretty clearly – but I looked back in my college journals and find I had written up another account in November of 1971 which was quite different from present memory! Was the earlier memory more accurate? It includes some significant differences. I'm going to try and research this – since I still have and find out which is the accurate one. At any rate, I copy the 1971 versions here:

> It seems I came near to killing quite a few of my
> friends in those days. One time Bob Culbertson had his
> cousin Franky visiting him. Bobby and I decided to
> take Frank up to the gravel pit between the depot and
> the dump, so we went most of the way on our bikes and
> then pushed our bikes up the last stretch of the steep
> gravel road. We hung around for a while in the middle
> of the afternoon and decided to go home after we all
> had our pockets full of pretty rocks.
>
> Franky got on the back of my bike and we
> started down the steep hill. It soon became apparent to
> me that I didn't have a great deal of control over the
> bike. By the time we got to the bottom of the hill we
> were really clipping along. Then we hit a truck rut and
> I, Franky, and the bicycle flew through the air and
> landed in that order. Apparently I didn't have so many
> rocks in my pockets, because I flew farther. The bike
> and Franky both landed in the same spot, however, and
> Franky landed on a pocket-full of rocks, neatly breaking
> his leg.
>
> Well, Bobby and I didn't believe him when he
> said it was busted, and we tried to get him to stand up
> and walk on it. He couldn't though, and finally I got
> tired of waiting, numbskull that I was, and went home.
> I found out the next morning that Bobby finally went
> down to Scott's lumber yard [at that same end of town]
> and got a ride to the hospital for Franky, where [no
> doubt after involving Bobby's parents] they put a cast
> on his leg.

Another time I was over at Tommy's house and Tommy
showed me and a younger friend, Jay Murphy, his new darts
board complete with three very sharp darts. We threw at the
board for a while, then decided to liven things up and began
throwing them at each other, sticking them in the walls, etc. It

was sort of a three-way war, with each of us hiding behind furniture until someone threw a dart near us, which we would recover and throw back. Finally I flung a dart just above the back of the sofa where Jay Murphy was hiding just as he came up for air and it stuck directly in the middle of his forehead. He started hollering and I charged up the stairs, leaped on my bicycle and headed for home. I was deeply relieved the next day to hear he had survived. There seems to have been a pattern there – I ran away from trouble and always got into more trouble that way.

[This story, too, I find I wrote up in 1971 with significantly different details, including Tommy himself being the victim I impaled, rather than Jay. Tricky things these memories!]

My friends (Bob Culbertson, Bob Ritchey, Tom Leinart, etc.) and I used to go up to the Fort Benton dump and bring home innumerable treasure of all sorts from that repository of human discards and wastefulness.

We would walk along the unimproved dirt road by the river at the northeast corner of town, down past or sometimes through the river bottom full of cottonwoods, and then up to the dump itself, where the side of the hill had been gouged out and levelled so that vehicles could back up to the edge and dump down the steep slope toward the lagoon below.

They say Lewis and Clark stood on the peak of the hill behind the dump, and looked down over the river and long stretch of river bottom that is now Fort Benton. Maybe it was only we who said it – perhaps with little basis in reported fact. I think we called it "Lookout Point," but it's more official name seems to be "Signal Point". "Charley Russell," as everybody in Montana calls him, painted a bunch of Indians looking down from there – or was it Lewis and Clark? Anyway we had many reasons beyond historical reminiscence to go down to the dump.

For one thing, we enjoyed climbing any hills there were to be climbed. From the top of "Lookout Point," there was a long slide down the flaky black clay slope – just dangerous enough to be exciting. At one point somebody came up with the idea of getting big pieces of cardboard from the dump and taking them up to the top to be used to toboggan down on. Pete and his friends may have been the inventors of this means of locomotion.

As in many of our expeditions into the hills, we would sometimes coagulate into "armies" and engage in deadly warfare, throwing chunks of clay at each other. Sometimes we rolled big rounded concretions down at great risk to the souls who might have been using the dump. The most successful of these launches were those that not only went careening down the hill but bounced in such a way that they shot across the levelled area and crashed down among the cans and bottles, perhaps going all the way to the lagoon.

That old dump (there's a more tidy one now to the west of the old) was started sometime in the dim past. It seemed large to me then, with nearly endless potential for discovering useful items discarded by others. We dabbled around among the recent discards at the top – crates, three-legged chairs, broken toys, logs, bottle still half-full of anonymous substances, and all sorts of thingamajiggers and figliggies in all states of repair. We gathered far more than we took home, and what we took home was seldom used for anything. We found hospital supplies, dead and decaying creatures, and many items we could not identify. A few times we found "girly magazines" which fueled my growing penchant for such things.

Bob Ritchey and I once spent a Saturday afternoon collecting parts of TV sets, boards, and other useful items, which we put in a large refrigerator crate. Somehow we thought we would be able to haul the whole load home – but mercifully our minds wandered to some other pursuit and our findings remained where they were gathered.

Sometimes we would grow bolder and climb down the slope made entirely of dumped debris – tires, cans, bottle, tree branches, lumber, appliances, etc. It was very unstable, constantly threatening noisy avalanches. On one such occasion Bob Ritchey cut his knee fairly badly.

A variation on rolling rocks down from Lookout Point was doing the same with old tires. Or if we were feeling lazy, we would just roll them down the lower slope of debris – producing a great deal of racket, and sometimes ending in a splash at the lagoon. We felt a certain measure of accomplishment as the last clinking and clankings of the settling trash faded into the still Montana air. Sometimes we would collect a bunch of bottles and fling them up in the air out over the debris slope, to be pelted with rocks, or more accurately – in an attempt to pelt them with rocks as they descended. Those that ended up in the lagoon we eventually sunk with our barrages.

Sometimes we would explore the river bottom below, just the other side of the lagoon. There were a number of wrecked car bodies down there. We'd go through them and remove anything that could be removed. One time I spent a couple of hours getting a nameplate off of one of them. It was blue and white enamel in a sort of cloisonné – nice before I set to work on it. But I bent it and broke the enamel, so I couldn't add it to Dad's old car nameplate collection as I'd planned.

When I was younger, Dad took us on an expedition around that area once or twice. I remember seeing hobo huts, often constructed in conjunction with an old car body. I recall Dad telling us about hobos and how they always drank muscatel. The railroad cuts back fairly close to that area and the hobos who rode the freights in the spring would camp there. One time we found one of their camping places with a couple of car-seat springs for beds, and makeshift curtains on the windows. There was a bed of ashes in the middle and a board nailed to an adjacent tree for a shelf upon which sat an ancient mason jar, full of what appeared to have once been carrots – no doubt salvaged from the dump. And sure enough lying nearby was an empty muscatel bottle. I hankered after hopping a freight myself some time, without a clue as to what sort of life that really entailed.

The lagoon tapered to sort of a creek which curved away from the dump separating most of the bottom from the road (rendering the bottom technically a peninsula). This shallow and narrow "creek" was a good place to hunt for various creatures. We caught frogs and tadpoles there which activity required getting well plastered with odiferous black mud from the not-so-fresh water. But the biggest and most exciting quarry to be found there were the carp. They wended their way into this finger of water and congregated in its pools. When we came upon them we would attack with rocks and clubs, or whatever other weapons we could find. We killed a few and caught at least one alive. They could be eighteen inches long and thrashed nobly. There was a kind of guilt I felt when we killed one, but it wasn't strong enough to prevent the next encounter. My father always emphasized mercy toward dumb creatures, as I have said, a "green" before there were greens.

The dump was inhabited by a number of skunks – and often smelled of them. One night my parents drove us up there in a car, and the headlights picked out a veritable swarm of skunks working through the recent garbage. The skunks used to come into town in spring or summer and get into altercations with the numerous dogs. These encounters always left a certain atmosphere to be detected the next morning.

Later, my brother Jon took on the mantle of dump-explorer. He was particularly interested in various steel and iron objects. He started a "metal collection" which was not as appreciated by our parents as it ought to have been.

Dad claimed that he once hauled a load of miscellaneous scrap to the dump and then went for a few errands. When he got home, all the things he threw away were piled up in the garage – additions to Jon's "metal collection".

Bobby Culbertson's house was down the 1900 block of Franklin Street with the biggest yard on the block. There was a lot of lawn to mow, especially on our side of the property where it abutted "Shorty's House". At the back of that part of the property near the alley and next to Shorty's garage was a big Taj Mahal of a rock garden. I remember Bobby's dad, R.J., who was our town postmaster, building it. The rusty and crusty cement mixer used in the operation sat around out back for many years after. The rock garden was a round, terraced, tower of a thing, originally designed to have water emerge from the tip of the tower and waterfall down over the various terraces. I recall seeing bleeding-heart flowers in that garden. I'm guessing the tower was 20 feet high, although my own boyhood height may lead my memory to error there.

Next to the rock garden, between it and Shorty's garage was a weeping willow tree, the branches of which made excellent whips in the hands of boys, but whips to be feared in the disciplinary hands of RJ. We boys used them mainly on each other and random dogs.

On the boulevard at the front of the property, near Shorty's driveway, was another tree, a boxelder, which had a branch over the sidewalk just made to swing on. More than one bicycle had years taken off its life when its pilot abandoned ship by means of that branch.

In that big stretch of lawn Bobby and I once spent part of the night (our Moms no doubt rounded us up around 9 or 10!) watching satellites until one of them turned a right angle above us and wobbled off toward the east. So it appeared to us. Thus we jumped to the obvious conclusion that it was a UFO full of alien invaders. After some discussion we became so convinced that we hid in the moon shadow of Shorty's garage under the willow tree, in hopeful dread.

Was it on the sidewalk near the boxelder that Mother berated and lambasted the wilted and nearly speechless R.J. after his boxers got loose and played tug-of-war with our short-lived cat Bootsy?

Bob and I were involved in many and sundry projects together. We set up as high entrepreneurs, selling Koolaid every summer. We never came close to making any profit, but since we seldom had any investment, we didn't take it too hard.

A couple times we became fascinated with the idea of manufacturing flavored merchandise. Once we bottled our own Koolaid, buying small medicine bottles from Ray's drug store for four cents each and filling them with Koolaid. It wasn't the Koolaid all our moms used, that came in square packets and made up a quart or two of summer-time drink per package. Rather it was the stuff in the long straws that was sold as candy, and tasted strong but awful. We stored our merchandise in the attic of Bobby's garage, which was one of many places to serve as a temporary "clubhouse".

That attic, in the rafters above RJ's workbench, contained various curios, including a tin roller coaster which, when wound up, was supposed to take tiny cars roaring up and down the hills and valleys – alas it did not work very well in its dotage. The attic always smelled of new lumber.

The other "flavor" project I recall involved three or four of us including Tommy Leinart. We used medicine bottles (the same ones?) and purloined doses of cooking extracts from our mother's cupboards. We put wooden toothpicks in each and let them soak up the essences, then fooled ourselves into thinking there was something pleasant about sucking on those toothpicks. As I recall now, mostly they left a burning sensation along with their strong flavor of lemon, clove, vanilla and what have you – no doubt mostly alcohol.

Culbertson's basement was another exotic place – somehow very awesome. There was a bar down there, with a mirror and a row of miniature bottles, and there was (what I was sure was an illicit) figure of a naked lady holding up an ashtray on the floor. Also there were big chairs and a couch as well as a couple of bar stools. It was always sort of dimly lit there, and had the slight odor of detergent from a washing machine that frequently over-flowed in the next room.

Upstairs, there was a very big living room with a fireplace at the front. Above the fireplace in the center of a wide mantle stood a statue of Jean Lafitte – noble, militant, though somewhat tattered in dress, and oh so buccaneer! I know that statue was one of my ideal images of masculine attainment and deportment for many years!

Out behind the property and across the alley Culbertsons had another big lot with a large garden and corn patch, as well as a big dog-pen. In that garden Bobby taught me how to fight the rototiller, and I have many memories of the dog pen. The fence around it was tall and originally well built, with an electric fence near the bottom. RJ had a bunch of boxer dogs. I've wondered if he'd brought the original pair home from WWII. In any case they multiplied and I recall as many as seven grown dogs at a time. In my eyes they were equivalent to wild lions. Thus Bobby was equivalent to a lion tamer when he entered that pen to do the chores of feeding and clean-up. The "lions" were prone to digging – thus the interior of the pen was quite a dramatic landscape of holes and hills. (I think the occasional escapes were due to this burrowing habit.)

The lion tamer's ritual involved first removing all the braces and latches from the door, then the task of making enough noise, offering threatening gestures, etc., so that the lions backed away from the door long enough for the tamer to slip through before any of them slipped out. Those great short-haired, lean, tanned creatures were noble but also savage, as many in the neighborhood knew. Chickens, cats and small dogs were very likely to fall victim to a loose boxer.

The favorite dog, perhaps the original, was tame enough that she spent considerable time outside the cage, albeit often on a chain. She was called Kickendorf. It seems to me I was told Patty had come up with the name, and there was some kidding (I never knew if it was malarkey or not) that this was Mrs. Culbertson's maiden name. Kickendorf was loved and kicked indiscriminately, depending on her behavior and her owner's mood. The boxers were all removed and/or sold a few years before the Culbertsons left. As long as he was there, however, Bobby always had a dog.

One time one of Bobby's dogs got loose and into Mrs. Ayer's chicken yard, where it killed some chickens. Mrs. Ayers lived across the street from the Culbertsons. Her husband, "Mr. Ayers," to us, was an old farmer and a grandfatherly friend. We visited him to hear stories about his farm and tractors. Mrs. Ayers, however, was extremely defensive about her chickens, and though a kindly soul, she drew the line with them. Bobby's dog having killed her chickens, Mrs. Ayers informed the Culbertsons of her great displeasure. Mrs. Culbertson sternly told Bobby to go apologize to Mrs. Ayers. I was not interested in going along.

Afterward Bobby told me he had gone across the wide street and up the long sidewalk to the front door, where summoning all his courage, he rang the front door bell and was solemnly admitted. He then told Mrs. Ayers he did not mean to let his dog get into her chicken pen, and he hoped to keep his dog from ever killing any of her chickens again. Whereupon Mrs. Ayers, good Baptist that she was, burst into tears and hugged him, and said she was sorry, too, and gave him a kiss – embarrassing him no end. At the time he was a bit tongue-tied, but very expressive recounting it to me.

Neighborhood friends: Holmes girls, Jim Berg, Tom Leinart, etc.

CRUEL HEARTS AND KIND

Others of my friends and kindred had dogs. Tommy Leinart had a German Shepherdish dog which he named "Rinny" after the TV dog hero Rin-Tin-Tin. Rinny was a good dog, but high strung, and a gang of boys were not beneficial as dog-trainers. We used to tease Rinny to the point of frustration, all except Tommy who tried to get us to treat Rinny more gently. Alas we did not, and I believe eventually the poor creature had to be put down – possibly Bob Leinart took him up to the dump and shot him. There may have been talk of taking us to the dump and shooting us, instead, but Rinny lost out.

Our sins were many and there was more than one thing for which the group of us deserved some punishment we did not receive. There was a lady who lived all by herself on the other side of the alley beyond Culbertsons at the end of the block. Her name was Mrs. Reicks.[5] Her house was a two story gray frame. She had a couple of sheds, including a chicken house and chicken yard. I can hardly think of her without feeling guilty, because early on through those idiot imaginations and communications of small persons, we decided she was a witch, and quickly convinced ourselves and each other it was a certainty. All we knew of witches was from Hansel and Gretel and like stories – they were reputed to be malevolent old ladies, who tried to do harm to people by magic – especially to children. Most of our sins against her were unknown to her. But there were a few occasions when we hollered something from behind a hedge as she made her

---

[5] Elizabeth Reicks, 1887-1978.

way home along the alley. We threw rocks at her chickens at least once, which when you consider it, is not the best way to avoid being bewitched!

My mother caught wind of our attitude toward her and straightened me out as to facts – I'm not sure that changed my outlook. Having studied the Salem Witch Trials of 1692, I am horrified to think a less enlightened adult population could have believed our benighted reports and ended up hanging the innocent lady – as 19 innocent persons were hanged at that time! I still feel a bit guilty and am thankful we and Mrs. Reicks did not live in seventeenth century Massachusetts!

Across the alley from Mrs. Reicks, on our side and at the far end of the block lived Mrs. Small. She was more of a Mother Goose in our small minds. We would go over there in the spring to see the baby chicks she brooded in her basement. In the summer her high-hedged back yard was full of fragrant, and later, tasty green apple trees. Like most of the other yards in the neighborhood, hers had a vegetable garden, and flowers: hollyhocks, lilacs, and honeysuckle. Sometimes she would send us home to get bandannas, which we would bring back so that she could wrap up a cookie or three in each one, then tie it to a stick –and send us out "on the road" as hoboes for the four or five minutes we could hold off before sitting down to eat the cookies.

Merlin Ulrich was another kid who Bobby and I looked upon as an equal, although he was only around for a few years before his family moved first to the far end of town then away to Lewistown. Merlin was famous in my family for a saying "I goin' bi' you," which translated meant "I'm going to bite you." If Merlin was incensed, one had to protect his extremities. "I goin' bi' you!" was a kind of battle cry, indicating he was on the warpath. My specific memories of him include an Easter egg hunt in our yard in which he, Bobby and I all hunted for the Bunny's trophies. I think the memory was supplemented by an 8 mm movie. I also recall being cautious during some period of time about going into his home (the basement apartment at Culbertsons) because his sister had polio, which was advertised as pretty scary in those days.

Licorice pipes with Cuz Dave & Howard & Darrell Holm.

A few years later all of the classes at the elementary school (and junior high) were marched down to the gymnasium where we were given a lump of sugar with a pink spot to eat and thus prevent us getting polio.

Tom Leinart's grandmother, Mrs. Vanhorn, lived across 19th Street from us, and was another benefactor of the neighborhood youngsters. Her husband, T.B. Vanhorn, owned Power Motors, the Ford dealer in those days. Mrs. Vanhorn gave us t-shirts with new cars emblazoned across the chest, and often provided various refreshments, which we took too much for granted. (Curiously, we had Vanhorns living on both sides of us, but Dave, "Shorty," was not related to T.B.)

The T.B. Vanhorns had a wonderful vegetable garden and a tool shed, which was one of our "Club houses". The garden was the best source of raw carrots in the neighborhood. Their apple tree, too, produced a fine apple, tinged with red in the fall. Our interest in agriculture was not always appreciated as it was observed that when replete, we continued to harvest apples for use as missiles. T.B. taught his grandson Tommy and me a lot about fishing. I recall he always kept a plug of tobacco in his tackle box, which in my teens, I sometimes availed myself of.

T.B. Vanhorn and me and a mornings' catch.

Other popular sources of fruit in the neighborhood included our crabapple tree, our plum trees, Culbertson's plum tree, one of Culbertson's apples (the rest were "pie apples" – too sour for us) and Small's apple trees. Much of our harvest from Small's and Vanhorn's took place on dark evenings.

Our own apple tree produced small oval crabapples that turned bright red in the late summer and made the world's best syrup and jelly. They were good to eat, too, but only when very ripe – and always with a pucker.

That tree was in the back yard next to the garage. We built a tree house (our parents let us build a tree house!) at what seemed a precarious height then – something like six feet off the ground. There we held some "club" meetings, during which we wondered vaguely what a club was and what one was supposed to do in a club meeting. One time Carolyn Holm from down the block fell out of our tree house and landed on her back – and gave us a few moments scare while she struggled to catch her breath – at last succeeding to our great relief.

Another somewhat more formal and dignified club was "the Green Garage Club," which may have been founded by my brother Pete. He had a lot of good ideas and I had no shame then (though more vague guilt now) over appropriating them. The Green Garage Club met every time two or more of us got together in our garage to add to or subtract from the treasury, and candy collection, which somehow remained always near a deficit, but which proved there was value in a club. I recall these assets were important enough that I would occasionally check them even without a quorum present.

There were other tree houses and club houses, though none were long-lived. For a while we "met" in our own toolshed, an ancient building with mysterious tools of all sorts hanging on the walls as frameworks for spiders. It was small, nestled in shrubbery and far enough from the house to be "secret". There was also a small cubby-hole built into a corner, an excellent place for hiding valuable possessions. (I suspect this little box may have been used originally to keep poisons in, back when arsenic in the form of Paris green and such things were commonly used – since it was high and had a door on it. Indeed for years there was a mason jar with Paris green in a corner – about which we were sternly warned.)

Our toolsheds and the Vanhorn's served another important function. Their roofs were great places to jump from. Jumping was a great challenge, as I guess it has been for boys since time immemorial. However we had the added incentive of watching movies of paratroopers and cowboys jumping off roofs and from trees on their adversaries. These things we had in our imaginations as we jumped the six or seven, or eight feet from those tool sheds. Jumping showed up in some of my recurring dreams.   Freud notwithstanding, we enjoyed jumping. By sixth grade both Tom Leinart and I had knee trouble – something they called Osgood Schlatter's disease, and I've wondered if all that jumping didn't contribute to it.

Other families in the neighborhood who furnished good friends and buddies to me and my siblings included the Aznoes and the Scotts.

Bobby Culbertson and I were always proud that our first "meeting" took place in the form of a rock fight.   And I believe Donald "Donny" Scott and I began our close association in the same manner. He moved in across Franklin Street (in a house since demolished when the Goods built their house) and we took advantage of the graveled street of those days to pelt each other from our respective yards. After doing a little damage to each other, it was natural we would feel kindly disposed and we were good friends from then on. Donald was athletic and as soon as he moved in, we began to play football, run track, and to wrestle (which we always had done, but without realizing it was a "sport").

Bobby Culbertson's family moved to California when I was in seventh or eighth grade, and I've only seen him twice since – once with his wife and sons, who look a lot like him!

The wonder of it is that we never killed each other. I came awfully close to blinding one friend, however. Bob Ritchey, the Methodist preacher's son became my "best friend" after Bobby Culbertson moved to California. He and Tommy Leinart and I hiked over the hills behind town and down to the old farmstead that used to lie in the valley beyond. There was no house there, but an extensive corral with some barns and sheds and haystacks. We all had BB gun rifles – and somebody took the first shot that started a three-way war.

We ping-ed away at each other and scampered about from cover to vantage point. Tommy ran across the corral and Bobby who was on top of a haystack fired and hit Tom in the leg. Tommy hollered ouch and Bobby opened his mouth and laughed, at which point I fired from behind a fencepost, and hit him on the <u>inside</u> of the cheek! Now the horror of this is that Bobby only had one good eye! Three inches higher and we would have had to lead him home by the hand! I imagine we were ten or eleven at that point, and I think the reality of the risk began to dimly sink in at that point, and we ceased fire.

Bobby Ritchey, another best friend, recently departed.

When I think of how close we came on many occasions, I can only thank God for divine protection. In the last few years my oldest two Trott cousins revealed a sobering tale to the rest of us concerning our grandfather, Gustavus Shepherd Bean Trott, the last of perhaps ten generations of Trotts born in Maine, whose father had moved to Andover, Massachusetts. Gus, at the tender age of 20, had accidentally killed a 37 year old father of four children. According to Joy, and to Karen, who subsequently found a newspaper account, Gus was haunted by this fact even into his later years. The fact, incidentally explained something which always puzzled me as a boy – that my father did not like hunting. In reflection I found this all the more striking when I remembered he had once taken a couple of us out to Spring Coulee where he went through the motions of trying to get a pheasant with his shotgun – for the sole purpose, I am now convinced, of letting his sons know hunting was OK if not particularly worthwhile. But thanks be to God that we never killed anyone. There was one fellow we knew from Fort Benton who accidentally killed a friend with a 22 rifle, and it seems to have deeply affected his life.

Like most of my peers, I was given a 22 rifle when I was eleven, and enrolled in a Hunters Safety Course, which met up at the rifle range at the north end of town. After that, we frequently went hunting rabbits (snowshoe hares or jack rabbits) on winter weekends. I went bird hunting on a few occasions but only remember getting one Hungarian pheasant and one Chinese pheasant, the latter which was contested by Tom Leinart since we had both shot at it before it came down. I have never shot a deer, although I have butchered five or six, and we really like venison! I should add that largely as a result of the Hunter's Safety Course, and partly due to a few family stories of firearm misadventures, we did indeed take gun safety seriously by then – never pointing our weapons at each other, and crossing fences very carefully, etc.

When my Uncle Norris Hanford (or possibly Howard?) was a lad, and the family was dwelling at the Highwood farm that became the Robinson's place, he walked into the kitchen one day from bird hunting carrying his shotgun rather nonchalantly and his mother, Grandmother Louise, told him to take that gun out of her kitchen. He told her, "Don't worry, mother, it's not loaded," and proceeded to demonstrate by firing it into the ceiling!

After Bobby Culbertson moved to California, Bob Ritchey may have been my official "best friend," but in actuality there were several, including Tom Leinart, Kent Aznoe, Don Scott, Jim Herbold, and later, Rocky Highfill.

Kent introduced me to and involved me in the world of rocket science, some of our experiences of which I will describe at more length later.

That other "best friend," Bobby Ritchey, was only around for a few more years. His father, George, was the Methodist minister, and I think they were the last minister's family to reside in the old parsonage next to the Elementary school. I recall a few events in that parsonage – including a snapshot or two of the Roger Robinson family (not related to our cousins, the Francis Robinsons.) It was a surprise to me to find my wife had heard of Olive Robinson's family – specifically her father, Roland Bainton -- a nationally respected church historian, who wrote about the Reformation and Martin Luther. It's a small world.

(Other such Fort Benton claims to fame go with a doctor who practiced a while in town, one of Hemingway's sons, and a high school principle who was a nephew of the famous missionary wife, Elizabeth Elliot.)

I think Bobby Ritchey must have showed up when I was in 4th or 5th grade. I know he was there in 6th grade when I had my one and only public brawl, and it was a strange one. In my 6th grade class, taught by the other Bobby's mom, Ella Culbertson, I had several good friends, including Danny Patterson, who used to bring "peppinos" red hot little dried peppers to school for us to test our manhood on, and had a complete set of Hardy Boys books he was willing to share. Also in that class was Mary Beth Taylor, of an evangelical family which helped found Community Bible Church in Fort Benton. She regularly brought missionary novels to school with hair-raising stories about Christian missionaries going into the deepest jungle where witch doctors attempted all kinds of evil against them, but the missionaries always triumphed by faith in the end. Being quite "religious" as my

89

own family was (we did everything Methodist there was to do) I enjoyed these books without giving much thought to anything but the stories. Yet, again, in retrospect six years later, I felt Mary Beth's books were used by God in my life – at least to make me a little more susceptible to genuine spiritual considerations.

But getting back to my one public fight, in that same sixth grade class was Tommy Hunter, who was a year or two older than I and was very "cool". He was one of those people (there were several such in my school career) who could mutter a funny line and get everyone round him laughing while he himself showed nary a sign on his placid physiognomy. We got along fairly well before and after, but at some point Tommy and I went up against each other and he challenged me to a fight, which I could not very well turn down. I could not turn it down because that would have been the basest cowardice, but the simple fact was I was terrified at the prospect.

Six or seven of the cooler sixth grade boys were informed of the upcoming event, and Bobby Ritchey volunteered his front yard next to the school as the arena. Tommy was by far the best bet to win, and I think that was the universal expectation. That I had a chance at all I think I owe to my sparring partner, brother Pete and those neighborhood friends with whom I often wrestled. I was nonetheless certain of defeat, and only hoped that by being "game" I might achieve a measure of respect despite it. No, I think it would be more honest to say I desperately feared defeat, because I expected to be maimed in the process. So the boys gathered, no ground rules were mentioned that I can remember. We began to wrestle, immediately tangling and dropping to the ground, where I immediately applied the one strong hold I had developed with brother and friends, a leg scissors with locked ankles across Tommy's belly. I applied the pressure with every ounce of my strength until he began to holler in pain and quickly "gave up". My terror had made me desperate and my "status" thus leaped far beyond my deserts.

Bobby Ritchey and I often went hiking together, caught scorpions and Black Widows in the hills, and went out to the Teton River during the summer where several times we lashed together driftwood rafts and floated down the dwindling stream a mile or two. Bobby moved to Harlowtown a couple years later, and we saw little of each other. The one exception was a week when he came back and stayed with us – the year the Teton flooded due to a broken dam far upstream, and we all drove out to witness the incredible sight – a stream thirty feet wide widening within a few minutes to fill the entire valley – half a mile wide!

The Teton flood – normally that bridge crosses the river!

Bobby shared with me on the phone, not long before he died, from his dad's journal. It seems his father considered me a good companion, but a bit of a risk-taker. My own father thought the same thing, and it puzzles me, since I have always known myself to be something of a coward, with no heroic self-image whatever. On the other hand, I did catch scorpions, Black Widows and rattlesnakes, which must have looked risky to others. It never seemed to me to require more than a healthy knowledge and a dose of deliberation in the execution.

Bobby got me in trouble with my Dad during that last summer stay. I think my Dad suspected me of living a double life for years thereafter. What happened was this. Bobby got ahold of "an old flame" (that's really my Mom's generation's language, but these things are fluid and written language borrows color wherever it can get it.) He actually got ahold of two old flames, Connie Thill and Raedene Nottingham, and arranged to meet them at the park (a few blocks from our house) after dark – at 8:30 or 9:00, I imagine. So that night we pretended to go placidly to bed in my second floor bedroom.

After the lights had been off for fifteen minutes or so and no more sound could be heard from the parents downstairs, Bobby and I slipped out of bed, got dressed and snuck into the bathroom, where I removed the screen on the window and we climbed out on the back porch roof. We then climbed down the big spruce tree that was at the corner of the porch and crept out of the yard, going over to the park. Sure enough the two girls were there to meet us, and Bobby assigned me to talk to Raedene while he talked to Connie.

Bob Ritchey and I during a visit (mid-60's).

And talk was what we did. It was a highly unromantic meeting. I suspect we were all so impressed at our boldness and even a little shocked by it, that talking briefly completed our agenda. We boys then high-tailed it back home, shinnied up the spruce, back into pajamas, and into bed. Just as we pulled the covers up to our chins, the bedroom light snapped on, and there was Dad. "Where were you guys?" he inquired. I don't think either of us were capable of replying. After a moment the light snapped off again, and we were left to meditate. I felt terrible over losing my Dad's trust – and resented Bobby's silly plot. It is a joy to report that he and I renewed our friendship over the last few years – he lived in Shawmut, Montana. We were both surprised to discover we both were trusting Jesus for forgiveness of a great many sins.

Raedene was another of those classmates with whom I shared almost all of my education, probably from kindergarten on up-. As far as I can remember, she was also my first formal "date." Were we in 5th grade? We met at the old Capital Theater, back when the Saturday matinee cost a quarter, and we sat through some movie together. In those days there was always a cartoon or two at the beginning, then an episode from some serial, like the "Iron Claw," or "The Blob" (functioning as serials do, to keep us coming back, no doubt), then the feature. It may have been a Jerry Lewis farce or a Cecil B. DeMille extravaganza. This was a pre-arranged date and we both felt terribly bold about it. I recall speaking with Clarice Holm in weary and worldly terms about how we fifth-graders were already "dating," while the sixth grade were behind the times.

Our teacher that year was Miss Cacchio, a dynamic, live-wire sort of a lady, who could occasionally get quite angry, and whose subsequent life had a number of very difficult points. During fifth grade I walked home down the alley with Rachel Vielleux. We always ran the last block before her house, which was on the same block as Jim Herbold's, and she always won the race – until the next year,

93

when I began to regularly win, and we tacitly agreed to stop racing. But not even by our senior year did I develop the ability to outrun her mentally or scholastically.

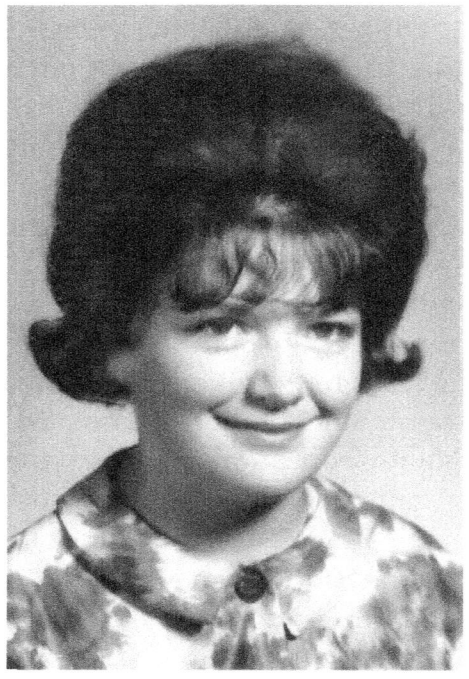

Raedene Nottingham, first "date," classmate and friend.

Seventh grade was outstanding in memory, chiefly because we were now thrown together with the brilliant eighth-graders and leonine ninth–graders, not only in the junior high wing of the school, but in romantic competition for the popular beauties in our own class. We wrote lots of notes to each other and passed them back and forth. I was honored to receive such written communications from Rachel, Raedene, Connie, Linda McClain, and sometimes from Bob or Jim. The subject matter was trivial, often someone's romantic inclinations – and at the bolder moments, a hint that one might even have some such oneself. Rachel tended to be the Beatrice of my Dante-ish imagination. I think we were sufficiently uncomfortable in one another's presence to indicate some mutual affection, at least during some of our time in junior high.

MYF (Methodist Youth Fellowship) became an occasion when I could sometimes walk Rachel home. Most of the kids in town belonged to their church's youth groups and these were a central social activity outside school.

Starting in junior high, Homecoming became a big event, and in particular, float-building, which involved each class, 7-12 grades, erecting some sort of colorful structure or sculpture on a farm truck bed representing the imminent victory of our own football team over whichever hated rival we were playing in the Homecoming Game that year. This took place in the late fall when the last warmth was absorbed as precious by everybody in the little town. Some were out raking and burning leaves, while some were digging bulbs or potatoes. Meanwhile farmers were at work at fall plowing and seeding, and students were building floats. These were constructed under cover in one of the large sheltered areas available, in lumber yards and fairground buildings.

When completed, the floats were driven down Front Street as a central feature of the Homecoming Parade which also featured the Homecoming Queen candidates (one from each of the high school classes), antique cars, the high school marching band, the mounted sheriff's posse, horse-drawn conveyances, various fraternal organizations, including the Great Falls Shriners in their little cars, kids from all over town in decorated bikes, trikes, and wagons; color guards from Malmstrom Air Force Base, and so on.[6]

It was a year or two later that my Dad took me aside and said, "you know, a little kissing never hurt anybody." I'm not sure that's the best advice for every young man, but for me at that time it was a blessing, and a liberating one.

---

[6] Pete says I am combining elements of the annual Fourth of July with the Homecoming parade here.

About the same time, possibly even that same week, I found myself a strange chaperone in that same fairground grandstand while a female classmate sat with a "practice teacher," a female teaching intern, while the two of them had a long talk. I sat down near the bottom, while they sat up at the top. I was there nominally waiting until after the "talk" to accompany my classmate home. She told me a few years later that the "practice teacher" was "gay," the first experience I had of homosexuality, although I hardly even had a category for it at the time. After she told me this, I had a peculiar mixed sense reflecting on my cluelessness and yet reflecting I may have been useful despite that. Perhaps I may have indeed functioned as an inept guardian for my friend.

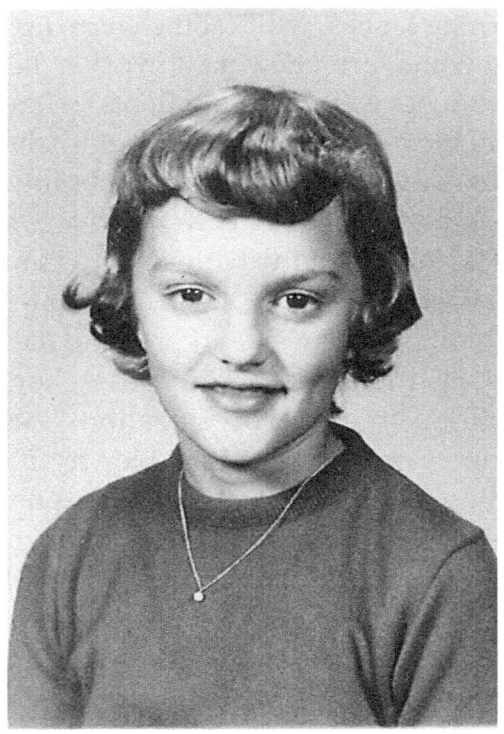

Rachel Vielleux, good friend and my "Beatrice."

Up into junior high, we used to spend a good deal of time running around in the hills near town – four sets of hills: 1/ those behind town, a range standing alone so to speak; 2/those across the river on the east side of the Highwood road, behind the "B" ; 3/those across the river on the town side of the Highwood road including the very high "bluffs" across from the fairgrounds, etc.; and 4/those down behind the old dump, a stretch historically known as Signal Point or "Crocun du Nez". Our activities included fashioning various "hide-outs," usually in the form of caves, from which we lunched forth against our "enemies" mythological or substantial in the form of other "gangs" or "armies," composed of our friends or relatives.

One time during grade school years, two of my buddies and I were over fooling around at a frog pond near the far end of the Old Benton bridge. After we'd gotten good and wet, and plastered with a certain amount of smelly mud, we went back in the trees to look around. And there Mr. King had a sheep pen. As we were walking tightrope around the top boards of the sheep pen corral, Mr. King drove up. He wasn't too happy with us being there and he proceeded to ask if were the young fellars who had been over the week before and chased his sheep and tangled them up in baling twine. We fiercely and fearfully maintained we weren't. But as we were walking back along the river bank to cross back on the bridge, certain of my companions allowed as to how that was a close one – because they were indeed the culprits! All the farmers and ranchers who had fields and livestock in the immediate area of town were pretty grouchy about kids fooling around on their land, and they had good reason to be.

Later in junior high, Bob Ritchey and I used to spend a lot of time in the hills behind town and down in the far valley beyond them. This was also the site of the BB war among Bob, Tom Leinart and myself as described above. There used to be some cattle sheds near a spring over there, a corral, an old slaughter-house, and often a haystack. Bob and I went over there nearly every weekend one fall. We got the bright idea of building a neat little hide-out in a haystack. We arranged the bales so there was a little room in the middle, with a small window and a hay bale door. Bob brought his comic books over and we'd just sit there and listen to the wind whistle and rustle the hay fairly comfortable down out of it and sheltered there. One time we invited a couple of girls from our class over, but they were not too impressed. It never did feel quite as exclusive after that! We often took our BB guns on these expeditions and knocked off sparrows.

Both Mom and Dad were instinctive naturalists – always noticing plants, animals, birds and insects and endeavoring to classify them. Thus it seemed normal to us to do likewise. Our adventures into the wild often included bringing back captive critturs, the more unusual the better, as I've mentioned. But we also picked up interesting rocks and even a plant specimen on occasion.

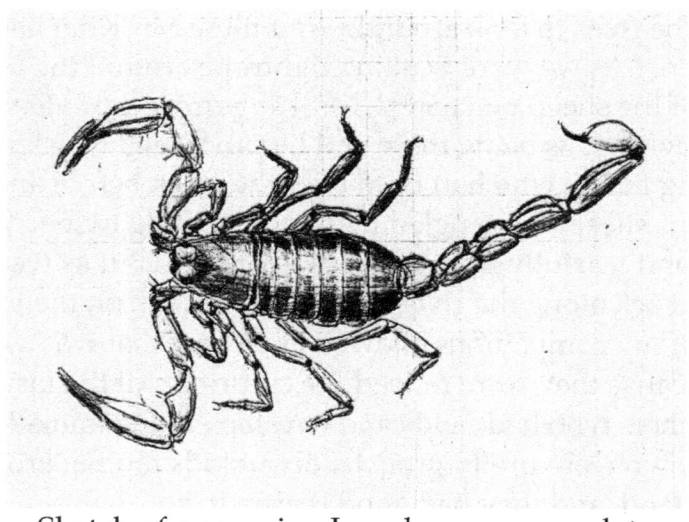

Sketch of a scorpion I made some years later.

I still recall the first time I found a scorpion. I had never seen one, in fact at the time I didn't think I'd ever seen a picture of one, but I had heard them described. It was probably 1959 or so, and I was digging into the cracked tan bank of a little gully, pursuing black widow spiders which were often abundant there – little males with their extra colors as well as the classic females. I was digging with a sharp stick, and I broke away a chunk, the equivalent of a shovel-ful of clay, which came tumbling down in a cloud of dust. I stood back to let the dust clear, and there on the slope below my excavations was a yellow and tan creature. "Scorpion" I said, calling on the Platonic type embedded in my mind.

I caught it in a jar, and perhaps two or three more that day. I brought them home, but my mother induced me to take them over to the high school, which seemed to me a lofty and unapproachable institution in those days. There I gave them into the care of Mr. Lepley, the biology teacher with whom I was to have much to do in future years.

Another time, on another solitary hike some few years later, I went up along the railroad tracks around "Signal Point". In those days the tracks came through town from Loma and on up to Great Falls. (It was mostly during the 1970s that the Milwaukee Road abandoned thousands of miles of unprofitable track, leaving little towns like Loma and Shonkin with no line. Thus that line dead-ended at Fort Benton.) It must have been late fall, because it was brisk and the foliage fading. I hiked away from town a good ways and then came back. Just as I passed a little line-shack by the tracks I saw a bird in the brush nearby.

It was the smallest owl I'd ever seen. I thought it must be a baby, although a more knowledgeable person would have recognized the season was wrong. I walked very slowly in front of it and it followed me with its big eyes, but with no evidence of alarm.

When I was only twelve feet away or so, I stopped and looked closely. It struck me that it was too calm for a wild bird, but I had an idea. I went on down the track thirty yards or so, then cut off the tracks and made my way as quietly as I could back parallel to the tracks, until I was behind the little owl. I then painstakingly moved toward it one very slow step at a time, expecting it would hear me and take off any second. But no, I got right up behind it and realized it might be possible to catch it. A saner person would have reflected that in general one does not grab raptors, because raptors are liable to grab back! But as swiftly as I could, I reached out and grasped it about the middle, figuring it might do some damage with its beak, but its claws would thus be immobilized.

The amazing thing was that even then the owl did not appear frightened! It didn't struggle or cry out, but merely turned it big yellow eyes on me as if to ask, "now what are you up to?" I was very excited. I thought what a great pet this would be, as I wrapped a neckerchief loosely around it. But then I began to reflect. How could it be this calm unless it was too immature to know better? Or perhaps its lethargy was due to being sick. I put it inside my coat and zipped it up to keep it warm. But I continued to worry. I had lost many wild pets over the years due to my ignorance of what they needed to survive. This little owl was so cute that I hated the idea of ending its life for it.

Cousins and friends at Robinsons with Pete, Andy and me.

So finally I came to the conclusion I needed to let it go on the off-chance a parent was still feeding it, or at least, that it would have a better chance of surviving whatever it was troubled by on its own in the wild. So I unbuttoned my coat, unwrapped the bandana, and let it go. It flew a short distance and alighted on a bush to stare back at me again.

Back home I looked it up in the innumerable nature guides my parents collected over the years. I found that it was a Saw-whet, a pygmy owl named for the characteristic sound of its call – like an old fashioned saw-sharpener with short strokes of the file on each tooth making a series of short, high-pitched notes. It was fully mature. It was not sick, but rather of a species that is notoriously unruffled and calm in demeanor. Thus I had a sense of loss over letting it go – but of course it was a loss for the better.

The family in front of the old gravesite memorial for Shep at the North end of town –photographer, Mom.

JET Family reunion at Swan River, 1997.

A view of the farm house from across the big reservoir.

THE FARM

After a short while in Chicago, where they met and first set up housekeeping, my parents moved to Montana, where Dad, at the advanced age of 29 took up farming. He had lots of support. My grandfather carefully gave a substantial chunk of farmland, not to Dad, but to Mom and her children – in case he turned out to be a scoundrel, no doubt! Farming nearby were also our kindred, the Longs, Hanfords, Robinsons, and Dyrlands as well as our friends the Rettigs to offer advice and equipment at need. In addition Don Knudson, Henry Grossman and the Glascocks were cooperative close neighbors on the Shonkin bench.

The farmhouse with the WD9 and one-way disc plow.

Although much of this memoir focuses on "fun" and the extracurricular activities of our family, as do many of the photographs included here, farming was Dad's fulltime occupation, and by our early teens, was the chief summer activity for the rest of us. Ours was a dryland (non-irrigated) small grain (wheat and barley) farm in a part of the country where 20 inches of rainfall per year (mostly in the form of snowfall) was considered a good average.

We had some very bad years. I can recall at least one dry year when Dad didn't even bother to harvest the barley. In the early days 25 bushels per acre yield was considered good. Now they often get 75 or 80 bushels, and considerably more in the best fields.

In addition to the continual potential for drought, bad insect infestations, and various noxious weeds, there was also the threat of hail, especially near harvest. These, with grain prices and escalating costs, were constant concerns for the farmers. There were various insurance policies available to the farmer, but of course they weren't free.   In the case of hail insurance, although Dad had some hail damage over the years, he figured he came out ahead by not buying any.

My folks could be light-hearted about the strangest things. I remember once after hail hit the home place, they had us gather up the hail and we used it to make ice cream in our hand-cranked freezer!

Other worries for the farmer had to do with equipment, which was complicated and undergoing as many or more changes as car models each year. The farmer could have his equipment repaired by the dealers, but most farmers did most of their own repair, and so had to become skilled mechanics. Some went beyond this and modified and improved their equipment with inventions of their own. My Uncle Norris was famous for these skills.

The countryside got awfully dry toward the end of an average summer, and the danger of fire was high as the fields ripened. I believe it was Wallace Stegner who argued that the Great Plains weren't really meant to be dwelt upon, much less farmed. He and others viewed the "Great American Desert" as best left to the wild life, because the lack of moisture made it unfit for civilization.

The family after a hail storm holding up some of the ice balls.

We had some bad fires, too. Most farmers got to where they had fire-fighting equipment geared up and ready to hand – and they would all converge on any fire that got started within 20 miles or so. I have written at more length about Dad's fire-fighting heroics in *Halo Around His Shadow*, but since I didn't include this photo of our family after fighting a nearby field fire, I'll insert it here.

Labor was also something the farmer had to worry about. Casual farm laborers tended to be classics of irresponsibility, disappearing for several days after payday, only to return to the job hung-over and broke. I don't recall this ever happening to Dad, but it did to my uncles. Dad tapped unusual sources of labor. One summer he hired a young man from his hometown in Massachusetts. Another time he hired the Methodist pastor who had baptized most of us. He also hired a local man or two when available.

All the Trott men grubby after fighting neighbor's field fire.

He made cooperative agreements with farm neighbors wherein they would help each other at harvest. I remember doing this with the Glascocks and Knudsons, and with Robinsons, Longs and Rettigs. By the time we kids were in our teens, we became the hired men, and that was how most farm families worked it. Some of us worked part-time for other farmers who had no sons available at the time. That, too, was a common pattern, but daughters drove tractor and truck, as well. My uncle Burton once hired three young men of my acquaintance from Highwood. I don't know if they inspired one of his sayings, but they at least reinforced it. On the question of how much work you could expect from hired boys he said, "One boy is a boy; two boys is half a boy – three boys, no boys at all."

Work was the rule, but since we weren't running cattle, and there were lulls in the routines of a grain operation, our lives weren't all work and no play.

For the first ten years or so, Dad commuted to the farm from town. He drove the fifteen miles or so back and forth, and when it was the season for seeding or plowing or harvesting or equipment repair, he left before dawn and returned after dusk.

When I was ten, Mom and Dad hired some contractors to build a house out on the farm. They planned it to be as economical as possible, and ended up buying a "kit" house, of the sort made popular by Sears and Roebuck back in the day. Dad asked around and found a contractor who some folks considered reliable. Whether his better workers had gone elsewhere or he subcontracted the whole thing, we don't know, but Matt remembers Dad telling how the crew seemed to stop at the half-way point from Great Falls, that is at the Highwood Bar, every day on the way to work.

This may have been a slight exaggeration, but there were some things about that house – especially the foundation, that indicated something of the sort. The big center wall that formed the partition between the furnace room and the boy's bedroom, ended in the middle of a window. Like all the other windows, it was an operating basement window, except that with the wall ending in the middle of it, it only opened a few inches. Pete's bunk was right next to it, so he got the non-benefit.

The foreman had a problem I'm somewhat sympathetic to – his pants waist was too small for his belly – so he not only kept the top button undone, but his zipper pretty low, as well. Dad mused about this detail as typical of the nonchalance of the crew. Dad tried to remain patient but the lapsed time plus the dubious workmanship was getting to him. He was out plowing the field near the house one day when he witnessed either the very late arrival or the very early dismissal of the crew and he'd finally had enough. He went home that night, called the contractor, and read him the riot act. That crew got fired and a couple of more responsible fellows showed up, who finally finished the job.

Distant panorama, Trott farm from the north.

When my sister and her husband remodeled the house a couple decades later, they found Great Falls Select Beer cans in the attic. (Great Falls Select was a local brand, and enjoyed by all the local connoisseurs. Our science club once went on a tour of the brewery, where there was an open tap on the wall for the employees to refresh themselves. I'm not sure why they went out of business!)

We spent our first summer on the farm in 1959, the year Matt was born. From then on we moved out to the farm every year as soon as school was out and didn't move back until a day or two before school started again in the fall. It was technically a three bedroom house with two baths or rather one bath and one shower room. Laurie was given her own room, whilst the five boys had 2 ½ bunkbeds in another. These were all in the basement where a water pump kicked on every half hour or so to sooth one to sleep.

I have faint recollections of the farm before we began to move out there in the summers, that is, before the house was built. My oldest memories go back to when the only building included the wooden granaries, the chicken coop, three steel bins and the old wooden "shop". I remember being there once with Dad in the fall when the wind was whistling across the fields and through all the cracks in the dry boards of the shop. The floor was dirt and was musty with oily appearance as well as odor. I remember the model T truck, standing out in the weather, restored to running condition (but not in appearance) by Sandy Gibson, Dad's summer helper from Dad's hometown in Massachusetts. Where the house would later be built there was just a patch of native grass. I have a faint recollection of chickens in the coop, but I'm not sure if that is fact or fancy. We never had any after the house was built, so if there were some, Mrs. (Grandma) Knudson must have cared for them.

Aerial photo of the farm with senior Knudson's at upper right.

Mr. and Mrs. (Grandma and Grandpa) Knudson lived across the reservoir coulee. The collapsed remnants of their original house was nearer to our farmstead, destroyed by fire before my birth. I remember Dad sending me and probably Pete across the coulee along the entrance road to get a drink of water from Mrs. Knudson one summer. She quietly welcomed us in in her high thin voice, and pumped water for us right at the sink, serving it in a long-handled dipper. The first time I ever saw a weasel up close was a dead one Mrs. Knudson had killed as it went after her chickens.

I remember what seemed to me like an army of men pouring the concrete floor of the Quonset hut and smoothing it with gas-powered finishers. It seems to me it was dark before they finished. I think the Scotts did the construction. It was rumored among us that the footprint back in the corner of the concrete floor was that of Kenny Scott, whose death was a famous tragedy in Fort Benton. He and three other guys went hunting in the high mountains, and they came upon a grizzly bear in attack mode, so a couple of them shot it, at which point, wounded, the bear retreated into thick brush.

The men knew they could not leave a wounded grizzly bear out there to attack the next hunter, so they went in after it. The bear was lying in wait, and attacked again. Kenny got off a shot or two before the bear was right on top of him. The other guy put another several shots into the bear, then his gun jammed. The other two guys came along and finishing the bear with perhaps another 6 to 10 shots – all these high powered rifle slugs. But Kenny was pretty much done-in by then.[7] Our football field, Scott Field, was named after him. His son ended up being a teaching intern and assistant coach one year when I was in high school.

The wooden granary beyond the steel bins was rigged up as a makeshift weight room by Dad and Sandy. It had various chunks of cast iron for weights and ropes over pulleys (boards) by which the weights were hoisted. By the time we built the house, the wooden shop just sort of disappeared. I don't know what became of it. I did witness the end of the chicken coop and the wooden granary in windstorms.

I have vague images of the foundations of the house being formed up and poured. I believe Uncle Burton did most of the digging of the basement with his caterpillar.

---

[7] More extensive accounts of this event were published in the newspapers, and are still told by a couple of the survivors.

The farm had changed from the time the Knudsons farmed it for Grandfather, and then when Dad started farming but all told, it hadn't changed that much by the time we built the farmhouse.

When we were out on the tractor going around and around watching the furrow and the implements and the gauges and eating dust as we got sunburned, there wasn't really enough to occupy our minds, even counting the occasional jack-rabbit or swooping hawk. Although we were strictly encouraged to keep our mind on the business at hand, most tractor drivers seem to find something to do to while away the time. We would sing, whistle, yell, yodel, concoct jokes, memorize or in some cases, even read. I think I tried all of the above. Pete used to memorize poetry, notably Poe's "Raven".

Andy on the WD9 and Pete on the Gvi, both pulling one-ways

Often I'd come up with what seemed to me profound and witty sayings, write songs and stories, but often I'd forget them before I could get back to the farm and record them. Once I got on a kick of coming up with riddles about what various people thought of our country, based on a *Boy's Life* joke I'd read -- what do automobile manufacturers think of America? They think it's a "car-nation". My additions included: bankers – donation; roofers – tarnation; engineers – damnation; farmers – cor'n-nation; JPs- marination; air force pilots – abomination; archaeologists – ruination, and sewer workers – you guess!

I found the tractor a good place to compose certain kinds of songs, for instance "Big Old Mac," a lively trucker's song with the rhythm of the diesel engine driving it. The WD9 and Minneapolis Moline may even have contributed the musical key! In a similar way, the rhythm for "Away I Go," a sort of sea-shanty came, not from the waves on the Massachusetts shore, but from a half-speed version of the engine rhythms. "Big Wind's A-blowin" also has that diesel cycle behind it, I think. I wonder what the wildlife thinks of those human yowlings added to the machinery noise. Trying to hear oneself over the engine at full bore was sure a good way to build up your vocal chords. It may have not been quite so good for your musical ear!

Ink and brush drawing (from army days) -- the farm from the north.

Partly because Mom and Dad were such nature-lovers, and partly because they were all around us, wild "critturs" were a regular feature of our lives, including many that ended up as foster members of the family, from my earliest days.

The first crittur story I recall, I knew more as a story than a memory. Our attic at 1904 Franklin Street in Fort Benton was largely dedicated to storage, and much of that space was taken up by four or five large trunks full of memorabilia, which we had to deal with after Mom died. But I mention it because the source of those trunks and more was my Great Aunt Bertha Hanford Comegys, my grandfather's only sister, who lived in Oakesdale, Washington most of her life. When she died in 1949, her siblings didn't want the memorabilia, so her Montana nieces said they'd take it. Thus Dad and Uncle Francis were dispatched over the mountains, driving a grain truck to serve as furniture van.

Dad as mother coyote – sc Pete titled this slide!

On the trip back, if I got it right, they came upon a dead doe beside the road with a tiny fawn lingering nearby. I'm going to bet it was Dad's idea, but one way or the other they decided to bring the little orphan back home with them, keeping it in the cab and feeding it how?

The crittur ended up at the Long's ranch where it was named Bambi after the hero of the old Felix Salten story -- which was one of the earliest and most effective pieces of "green" propaganda to come along. Bambi grew to adulthood, as witness a number of photographs and some old 8mm film footage, but what became of that pet, I'm not sure.

The earliest wild pet I remember was a baby skunk that Dad brought home one evening from the farm. I don't recall how he came upon it – presumably someone had dispatched its mother. In any case it was the cutest little thing and no doubt we named it "Flower," again drawing on Salten's story. Alas, it did not live very long. I mentioned how my parents lavished great labors on each of our early Christmases, and made wonderful scratch-built gifts, one of which was a rocking horse, which still rocks to this day, and which inspired me to make copies for my grandchildren. We kept it on the screened-in front porch which was kind of a neighborhood playroom.

One day a girl from the neighborhood was rocking vigorously when the little skunk crawled under a rocker, and he only lived a few more hours with his injuries. I recall feeling quite indignant and outraged at her carelessness. But when I think of all the wild creatures that died under my tender care, I have to swallow any judgment I might harbor.

Eddie Simmons was a friend a year older who introduced the joys of herpetology. (I don't remember exactly when the Simmons family moved out of town, but I know Eddie was around long enough to become famous at the swimming pool for a peculiar sideways move he had as he plunged headfirst into the water, known as "the Eddie Simmons Dive," and much emulated.) He had a big tight cardboard box in which he kept several garter snakes. He would take them out and handle them and invite us to do likewise, so that I felt a garter snake was the ideal pet and dearly hoped to get one of my own.

Dad told me there were lots of them around the big reservoir at the farm. So I went out with dad one weekend when I was eight or nine and wandered around the reservoir until I found one. Gleefully I grabbed the snake by the tail and gleefully the snake bent back and bit me on the finger. I dropped it in shock! I thought all garter snakes were tame! It never occurred to me they could bite! They also have the nasty habit of deliberately defecating most foully when caught by the head (which is the only way to keep most snakes from biting you), but after the initial capture they tend to calm down and are fairly placid pets.

Correcting my initial approach, I did catch lots of garter snakes over the years, including at least one that escaped its makeshift terrarium in my bedroom in town. It seemed to have disappeared completely until that Christmas, when dad pulled down the various ornaments and decorations from the cupboard above the closet. Among them he found a desiccated snake mummy coiled in the corner.

And while garter snakes are fairly quickly tamed by a little gentle handling, I learned that some snakes are pretty much untamable. A few years later I caught a yellow-bellied racer, cousin to the blue racer, both of which can move at very high speed through the grass. I'm not sure where I caught him, but I have a dim idea that it may have been on one of the fishing expeditions Tommy Leinart and I went on to various farm reservoirs in the area where fish had been planted. The racer was very nervous when I caught him and continued to be very nervous even after I'd had him for a few weeks and handled him regularly. One day a few weeks later I reached in to his box and he lashed out and bit me. His lack of affection inspired a reciprocal feeling in me. I let him go after that.

Another wild "pet" that taught me a hard lesson was a shrew I caught at an early age out at the Long ranch. It was a least shrew, which is the smallest mammal in North America, and which is a very high energy little insectivore that feeds practically constantly. I caught it in a jar or something, brought it back to town where we rigged up a tall cardboard box with some grass and water in my bedroom. As I turned out the lights at bedtime, and got into bed, I listened to the poor little guy continually jumping in a monotonous effort to escape those confines. I went to sleep listening to the same noise. When I woke in the morning, his lifeless little body lay stiff on the floor of the box. According to what I later read, his metabolism was such that overnight he had starved to death!

Malibu, the pet antelope.

We were a little more successful with larger wild pets at the ranch. One spring we picked up a baby antelope – probably from Cousin Ron who, although an active hunter and pest-controller, tended to feel compassionate about little critturs orphaned by his efforts or by accidents. We called it Malibu (all our pets were invariably named). I remember it running with "the herd" of us kids. I think I have a photo of Dad feeding it with a baby bottle. I think we turned it over to our cousins the Robinsons, who later gave it and some goats to a conservancy outfit, which placed the critturs on Scout Island in Great Falls. No tragic ending dwells in memory – I know no more of its fate.

We got a baby coyote from cousin Ron at the beginning of one of those early summers at the farm. Laurie named it "Mita Cota," an Indian name which she picked up from a library book meaning "my friend". The first couple of weeks the coyote lived mostly behind the piano, poking his little muzzle out querulously, but essentially wary of anything and everybody.

Again there was a short period of bottle feeding, but solids fairly soon, and the little guy adapted himself to having a family of eight – but no more! Anytime someone else was visiting he went into hiding again. I can picture his rusty-gray face peering out from behind a telephone pole at any strange vehicle and its occupants.

Mita Cota "my friend." pet coyote named by Laurie.

Mita Cota was remarkably like a dog in some ways and in other ways very different. For instance, he liked to play, but his teeth were as sharp as needles – so even gentle play might draw blood. He had less sense of humor than a dog and took himself more seriously. One time I shot a gopher near the big reservoir and with my 22 rifle on my shoulder, was carrying the carcass hanging from my other hand as I walked back toward the farm where I had some vague notion of skinning it. Suddenly the gopher was snatched from my hand and there went the coyote lickety-split ahead of me. I couldn't catch him before he disappeared somewhere back behind the bins, where he no doubt enjoyed the catered meal!

Sometimes our cousins would come over and we would take sleeping bags out in the yard south of the house where we'd sit up watching "shooting stars" and the myriads of other lights that spangled a Montana sky at night. Mita Cota would stay out with us. One night we heard a pack of coyotes off in Ever's pasture to the east. When they howled, we answered back, and suddenly Cota joined in. We howled and barked for a while, until the distant antiphony died out.

We knew the coyote could not come to town. After school started and we had moved back in, Dad continued to report on Cota's presence around the farmstead until he faded away somewhere. We hoped he had kept his wariness of other people, but feared we might have made him a little too trusting of two-legged critturs.

However, the next spring a neighboring rancher met Dad in town and asked if we still had that pet coyote. Dad said no, he had pretty much gone back to the wild, to which the rancher replied that they had been rounding up calves and a coyote had come out and hung around pretty close so that they decided not to shoot it on account of it must be "the one the Trotts had for a pet," which made us feel good on a number of counts.

As I write about Mita Cota, I wonder what kind of interface there was between the coyote and Bart or a cat we had. I can only conclude these domestic pets must have died before we had the coyote. I see from photo notes that we had the coyote the summer of 1969.

The relationship between domestic and wild pets was not usually very good. One time Dad caught a big horned toad when he was out plowing. These marvelous prehistoric-looking reptiles were very docile pets and seemed quite content to live on a few insects, so we set this one up in a washtub with some sand and rocks and vegetable matter. But a few days after we got it, I went out on the back stoop where we kept it only to find our Siamese cat, Singe, in the act of hopping out of the tub. When I looked in, the horned toad was bleeding from one eye – obviously injured. I don't recall to what degree we consulted the parents as to what we ought to do, but the upshot was that we took the toad over to a patch of prairie and let it go, hoping it would recover in the wild and flourish minus cats. Later, I read in our *Little Golden Book of Reptiles*, that horned toads have a unique defense mechanism whereby they can squirt blood from the corner of their eyes to discourage predators! Who would have guessed!

Singe met her untimely death within a few years when she caught and ate a least weasel. As near as we could tell, a bone from the weasel must have gotten stuck in her throat and led to her demise. Least weasels were tiny little mustelids, measuring only six or seven inches long. Onetime my Uncle Burton went out to his barn after four or five inches of snow had fallen, and as he was opening the barn door, he saw a little ridge of snow popping up on the surface from some crittur burrowing along under it. Thinking it was a mouse, he stomped on it, but when he swept the snow aside, he found a least weasel in its winter cost of pure white.

I often heard a classic beast incompatibility story while growing up. It was told originally by Uncle Burton Long, who, followed by his son and grandson, was a classic story-teller. The story featured another cat, one of those semi-feral critturs which tolerate humans and even seem to like them at times, especially meal times. This cat had the habit of sidling up to any stationary human and rubbing against a leg. And whenever it did this, the cat would purr, and when it began to purr, its tail would stand straight up, as a sign of pleasure.

The cat's humans were trying to make a little extra money when money was hard to make, and the enterprise they hit upon was raising mink for their fur. Mink are another Mustelid, kin to weasels and ferrets, as well as badgers and wolverines. Ladies seem to like coats made from their fur. These mink were being raised in wire cages, which in this case, were kept in a shed, where the cages were raised up off the floor about the height of a cat, in order to clean up under them. Sometimes the cat would wander into the shed where the mink would carefully watch and follow every move the cat made, but the cat studiously ignored the mink. One day the cat followed the mink-farmer into the shed while the mink were being fed and watered, and when the human paused in conversation with a companion, the cat sidled up to his trouser leg and began to rub, and when he rubbed, he began to purr, and when he purred his tail slowly stood straight up.

All unpredictable and unfortunate as it was, the cat happened to have his hind end under a mink cage at that moment and SNAP, as quick as you like, the mink locked on to the unexpected adjunct to his lunch, which had suddenly appeared and held on as only a Mustelid can. The mink had hauled the cat's tail as far into the cage as it could, thus lifting the cat's hind quarters off the floor. The cat was yowling and spitting and scrabbling its front claws on the floor. The mink refused to let go of his end, and the cat couldn't let go of his unaided. Calculations didn't take long – the mink was worth more than the cat's tail. Surgery was necessary. And so the cat spent the rest of its life and was thereafter immortalized as "The Bob-tailed Cat".

Sometimes the tables turned on the humans. Dad used to tell us about the time back east when Uncle Walter got on the trail of a pesky squirrel which had been nesting in his attic. He chased the thing all around the house and yard, until finally, no doubt desperate as its capture seemed inevitable, the squirrel turned and chased Uncle Walter for a while.

Once, when he was fairly new in Montana, Dad saw a badger lumbering across a field, and Dad ran after it. The crittur ran down a coulee bank, and when Dad got there, he ran down the bank after it. Whether because he lived there, or because it was against his grain to keep running from danger, the badger then turned, at which point Dad ran back up the coulee bank. Badgers are notably ill-tempered critturs, a lot like their cousin the Tasmanian devil as depicted in the cartoons. One time Roseann and I were driving through Spring Coulee when we came on four little ones crossing the road. I got out to take some photos, and they turned on me hissing and gnashing, and I could tell they were serious!

Another time I was hiking where the prairie rounded down toward a coulee and suddenly I saw an adult badger maybe seventy yards ahead of me. The second it saw me, it turned and began to trot toward me. I felt a bit badgerish myself, so I kept on directly toward it, and sure enough, when I was within forty yards, it turned abruptly and headed off toward the coulee. I figured that when he first saw me, to the badger I was no more than my head bobbing over the curve of the hill. No doubt he felt he was more than a match for that little crittur, but as more and more of my length was revealed, he reached a revised opinion and decided to find smaller game.

Pete had one of those turnabouts around 1968. He was doing something over by the grain bins next to the little reservoir and he saw a muskrat climbing down from the top of the dam there, so he hot-footed quietly around and snuck down the bank behind it. The muskrat sat busily engaged and preoccupied with chewing on something half-way down as Pete crept up behind him. Not wanting to unduly startle the crittur Pete said a few gentle words like, "Howdy, Mr. Muskrat," to small effect, for the muskrat merely looked back over its shoulder and gave Pete the once over, then went back to his business as though this sort of thing happened to him regularly. A bit miffed at being so blatantly ignored, Pete took a step closer, in response to which the muskrat turned around and jumped on Pete's shoe squeaking ferociously. Pete shook his foot desperately, loosening the passenger in the process, and turned and shot back up the dam. The moral seems to be you shouldn't follow or challenge anyone you don't figure you could lick!

I kept white mice in my bedroom in town for at least one long winter. The chief memories are olfactory ones. Also white mice have the very disconcerting habit of eating all their young if they are feeling insecure and self-centered. In this they remind me of humans.

My brother Matt had some unusual pets. One time he found three green caterpillars in our scraggly trees, the kind with the unicorn adornments. He named them Luther, Lester, and Larry. I'm not sure either they or he could distinguish which was which. Before that he had a pet leech, with whom he shared considerable mutual affection. He called it Rufus Luke. Matt wrote a sentimental account of Rufus Luke's brief but not uneventful life, which he charged us a nickel each to read. Much earlier than I, he seemed inclined to memorialize his pets in narrative form. Previous to the leech, there was a diseased fly, name of Herby, whose end was not memorable, at least not to me.

There were four or five snake species that were fairly common on the Montana prairie. These included the bullsnake, the prairie rattler, the garter snake, the yellow-bellied racer, and (in the mountains) the western garter snake. Much rarer, at least in my experience, was the hognosed snake, also known as the "puff adder". One summer Pete found one by the Little Reservoir, and I traded him out of it for something, no doubt of lesser value. I kept the snake in a bucket on the Propane tank on the shady side of the house, and tried to get it to eat grasshoppers, worms, and various other condiments – to no avail.

When the time of the summer came when I was scheduled to go to Kings Hill Church Camp, I turned the care of my hognose snake to the tender mercies of Mom. When I got back, the snake was dead. Mom somewhat abashedly confessed that she had been so worried about the snake not eating that she had ended up force-feeding it a little toad soon after which it expired. I sort of held this over her head for the next few years, but one year I gave her a little silver frog pin with a note that I forgave her for killing my snake. My oldest daughter inherited the pin which she just showed me the other day on my 70th birthday, still complete with the box and my handwritten note!

We encountered rattlesnakes regularly, and were brought up with a continual awareness of their existence and potential presence – in tall grass, in burrows, under debris, under equipment, so that few natives of the area were ever bitten -- so few that the exceptions were well known. We did not so much fear as respect them! I remember a young girl who was badly bitten when she was walking through a wheat field and froze as a big rattler struck her several times. She got medical treatment within half an hour and ended up all right.

Lively rattler caught at Lost Lake.

We had several close calls. One time Pete and I and maybe cousin Dwight were walking along through grass across the fence from the field where Dad was cutting wheat. I think Pete was taking pictures with his camera, when I happened to look down just as he was about to tread all unawares on a coiled rattler. He responded with alacrity to my warning. We often found the reptiles around the farm buildings and bins. If they were within a mile or so of dwelling, we killed them, but otherwise left them alone – since they are a well-known vector for rodent control.

Rattlesnake coiled for action and sounding the alarm.

I discovered in a book about a man who collected museum specimens in Africa that a tablespoon of tobacco was all it took to kill the biggest snake! Sure enough, I found a wad of chewing tobacco would kill a rattler in a short time. One needed a certain measure of caution in introducing it to the reptile, but since they have no regurgitative reflex, once introduced, the poison does its job. Possibly they should add this to the warning label.

In the fall of 2010, during a brief time in Montana, I came upon the only rattlesnake den I ever saw. It was well out in the middle of a big virgin prairie, in what may have once been a badger or coyote burrow. I came upon it quite by accident after running into several rattlesnakes in a row, which was itself very unusual in my experience. It was remarkable enough to me that, I borrowed a camera and took Roseann out to see it with me. It's quite an eerie thing to see a pile of rattlesnakes ranging from four feet or more to little foot and half guys all tangled up and crawling leisurely over one another, with more outriders drifting in all the time – including one that was headed right for us, since we were between it and the den.

Rattlesnake den near Shonkin – the only one I ever saw.

Apparently no one has figured out how the snakes navigate back to the same den every year – whether by celestial calculation or some kind of pheromone trails, or what. Apparently shared body heat through the deep cold of our northern winters is the chief advantage accounting for this instinct.

During the summer before my sophomore year at college, I decided I was going to make some money selling rattlesnake belts at Harvard, so I killed and skinned maybe ten snakes, with a little help from cousins and brothers, and when I had the skins stretched and well dried, I persuaded Rudy Lusin, the Fort Benton shoe-maker to sew them on wide leather belts. He only charged me a couple bucks each, and I figured to make as much as six bucks profit per belt, but by the time I had given one or two away and worn one myself, and paid for an advertisement, I think I made thirty dollars from the enterprise!

Lost Lake, a rather spectacular horseshoe canyon near our farm, and reputed to have been a glacial Niagara Falls in days of yore, was an ideal place to find rattlesnakes. In fact, I would guarantee anyone I could find a rattlesnake or two there within half an hour. There are all kinds of rock formations and broken boulders among and beneath which they comfortably dwell and hunt for rodents. On separate occasions I had two unique experiences with rattlers there.

On one occasion I found a rattler under a large flat rock and succeeded in fishing him out with my walking stick. I tossed him about twelve feet away and darned if that snake didn't turn around and head straight back toward me. Quite contrary to the reputation of their Central American cousins the fer de lances, prairie rattlers are not usually that aggressive. I tossed him again, but again he headed back my way. Feeling a little nervous, I moved away and watched as he headed back under his rock – apparently it was homesickness, not revenge that motivated him

Another time after we had made our way down the narrow passage that allows one to descend through the hundred foot horseshoe cliffs to the lower slopes that lead down to the alkali lake, we came upon several rattlesnakes, and with the help of others, I caught two of them. (Someone else pinned down the second one with a stick while I got ahold of its neck and thus held the two firmly behind the head, one in each hand. Somewhere there's a photograph.

We had so many snake stories that I find I cannot recall the details of most that I listed in my college journal. Perhaps it's just as well as any story-subject gets old after a while.

Nonetheless I'll tell two more that I do remember. The first is an oft told tale at the Long farm, known as "The Tallahassee Kid." My version is a poor substitute for the Long's oral renditions, but such is the disadvantage of the written word.

There were five Longs, Burton, Marian, Ron and toddler Nancy as well as Ron's Uncle Lewis, travelling back home from a day excursion south of the mountains and they picked up a solitary hitchhiker. This was not considered dangerous in those days, although in this case maybe it should have been. (This was 20 years or so before a couple of crazed Californians killed and partially consumed some Montanan who had picked them up hitchhiking, which put a considerable kibosh on hitching in Montana for a while!)

The fellow turned out to be from Florida and had an unusual penchant they soon found out about. As they drove along, someone saw a rattlesnake crawling into the ditch, so they stopped, and Burton got out a shovel with which to kill it. Getting out of the car "The Tallahassee kid" protested, and said he wanted to catch it himself. He beat around the ditch until he found the snake. Skeptical but interested, Uncle Burton and Lewis stood by to observe. The "Kid" then crouched down close to the coiled snake and with his left hand extended, tried to get it to strike at him! The snake, however, was not accustomed to these procedures and refused to commit himself. Finally the Kid got a stick and pinned the snake down, picking it up by the neck close to the head and walked back to the car, expecting his ride to continue despite the additional passenger! At first Burton told him to go ahead and kill it, but the Kid wanted to keep it alive!

Well, being hospitable people, the Longs reluctantly agreed. The family members who shared the back seat, a five year old Ron and his Uncle Lewis may have kept their hands on the door latches the rest of the trip. But the Kid proceeded to try and calm everyone's nerves by relating how things were done in Florida. It seems that back in his neck of the woods near Tallahassee there is a factory that cans rattlesnake meat. This factory pays good cash for rattlesnakes as long as they are delivered alive. Florida has a reputation for big snakes, and the bigger the snake the better the cash. According to the kid this motivates most everybody in those parts to spend lots of time out in the swamp catching rattlers.

The Longs sharing an early Christmas with us, ca 1952.

Apparently the real professionals all have dogs specially trained to sniff out snakes. The snake hunter goes out with his dog and wanders and wades around until, rejecting all cottonmouths, copperheads, coral snakes and small rattlers, he comes on a rattler worth his while. As the snake dog points him out, the snake hunter approaches the venomous quarry and induces him to strike. This he does by using his left hand as bait or lure, so to speak, but when the snake strikes, the hunter turns the tables and just like lightening, grabs the snake behind the head with his right hand. This seems to have been what the Kid was trying to do with the snake currently in his possession.

The hunter then places the snake's head between his fingers and continues to hunt for another. He uses the same procedure, with obvious complications as his tally increases, until he has four snakes, one between each set of fingers, on his left hand. Then he catches one more in his right hand, and heads for the canning factory, where the payoff occurs. One can well imagine by that time his left hand and arm are a mass of writhing and hissing snakes coiled around it and weighing many pounds. Obviously the process of untangling and "letting go" of the snakes is somewhat complicated and requires the aid of at least one other person, but most of this was left to the Long family's imagination.

As the story proceeded, another roadside reptile was sighted, and by now quite curious to see what might transpire, all the Longs got out to watch. Unfortunately the snake was only a racer, but the Kid caught it and brought it along just to keep in practice. They continued on their way toward Geraldine as uneventfully as possible in such a travelling sideshow. The kid occasionally brought the two reptiles face to face and they both tended to get more excited over it.

They eventually let the fellow off in Geraldine, where he had a farm job, and went on their way toward Shonkin. The two-snaked Kid tendered his thanks. Uncle Burton saw him a while later in Benton. The Kid communicated somewhat sorrowfully that he had not been able to get another ride until he dumped his cargo. One wishes one knew how the rest of his stay in Montana went.

(I checked with Ron who was eye witness and found there were a number of things I got wrong. I was surprised at how many things I got right! But I've since corrected my version to conform more to the facts.)

As I said, Mom and Dad were always interested in the natural phenomena around us, from the smallest insect to the grand panoramas and atmospherics around us. I have written in *Halo Around His Shadow* about Dad's interest in light phenomena, so I won't retell the story of the Great Daylight Fireball of 1972 here. I was by then in the employ of Uncle Sam so missed this spectacular event. But many another wonder was pointed out and explained over the years for which education every one of their children is grateful.

Dad had been fascinated by pond-life as a kid, and he knew the names of just about all the critturs that we found during our hours of swimming and floating on the reservoirs: backswimmers, giant waterbugs, horsehair snakes, garter snakes, tadpoles, waterdogs, muskrats, Jesus spiders, etcetera.

Water sports (swimming, rafts, etc.) on the little reservoir.

Although I used a photo Mom took at the ghost town Granite, where we three oldest were using one, we never had a functional outhouse on the farm, because we moved there pretty late. We had a septic tank and a drain field from the start. However, all my cousins had working outhouses which were pretty universally used in the warm months, and used by most of the men in the winter. The reason was simply that we all had to haul every drop of our water from Highwood or

Fort Benton, and every flush was more water used. By the same token we learned to always stopper the sink when washing hands, and use only a shallow sinkful, and to shower quickly, shutting the water off after wetting down while soaping up – again to save water.

There were always plenty of outhouse stories. I remember listening with fascination to some older fellow relating a sure cure for constipation, albeit not one the patient desired nor the doctor ordered. It involved wrapping some thin copper wire around two small nails, one tacked either side of the hole in the seat. The wires were then run out the back of the outhouse, where the culprit lurked until an unsuspecting victim came out and ensconced themselves in place. The culprit (or culprits – conspiracies are more fun) then either attached the two wires to a charged model T coil, or to an old crank telephone, which he cranked – either source of electricity literally galvanizing the person sitting on the seat.

Other stories, even more dramatic involved the disposal of something highly flammable, like gasoline, down the outhouse hole, and a customer lighting up his pipe or cigarette as he relaxed – to a dramatic effect. The punchline in those stories usually was about the cooking or one's digestion.

But my favorite firsthand story on this subject is one of Cousin Ron's concerning a simple but effective practical joke played by some bored high school boys in Highwood during a school dance. It seems that the school there, like most rural schools then (and I might add, most today in the rural reaches of Belize) had a double outhouse, that is a divided building over a common pit, with both a boys' and a girls' section, each with its own door. The bored young men acting on a plan no doubt passed on from ancient lore, went into the boys' side where they waited as quietly as they could watching through a crack in the door until some unsuspecting maiden came out to use the facilities on the other side. When they judged she had made herself sufficiently comfortable, the chosen one of their number called out – down the hole on his side – "Pardon me lady, would you move over? We're painting down here!"

131

There was very little time elapsed before the door slammed shut and, looking out through the crack, they watched the fleeing victim hauling her clothes back into place as she hastened to the safer and saner precincts inside the school.

Various cousins with Grandmother, Dave & I as bookends, ca 1949.

Backyard photo – Probably Easter, 1962.

SCHOOL IN FORT BENTON

In the winter, the hills behind Fort Benton were a favorite place to sled. Not only was there a very long slope to ride down, but in many places there were natural terraces that made for airborne stretches during the descent. On a very successful run, however, one had to look out for the barbed wire fence near the bottom. "The hills" official use was as cattle pasture.

During my high school years, I found great satisfaction in the thrill of leaping down the hundreds of feet of bluffs across the river from the fair grounds. One could soar like a mountain goat. I wonder that my joints could handle it. The combination of factors contributed to the excitement: very steep descents, occasional ledges or points where one could rest or arrest oneself, the friable black clay which gave one good footholds, while at the same time giving away and allowing one a controlled slide. On the surfaces of these bluffs, especially at the little ledges or points one might find fossil Belemnites – "squid tips" or even (for me on three occasions) big lead "miniball" slugs from the days when the fort was indeed a fort, or perhaps from the days when the fairgrounds was an army bivouac.

As implied in that description, I would often go up in the hills solo if no companion was readily available. I wandered lonely as a cloud and much as Wordsworth must have, I sort of enjoyed my loneliness. Not only did it give me a rather lofty (Natty Bumpo) image of myself, but it allowed me time to meditate on the failure of the rest of the human race to appreciate me. And I suppose it was true then as it is now -- I do love the created world and enjoy basking in it.

133

Both my father and mother loved the created world, and would bend and gaze at a minute flower or stand and drink in a vast panorama. We had a lot of both in the world I grew up in – something about the prairie and the eastern side of the Rockies – a lot of small beauties in the foreground and a lot of great beauties in the background, without so much in the mid-ground.   I suppose most Montanans have some appreciation of the beauty around them, but my father being an outlander, had more than most, and my mother with the Romanticism of her mother's side of the family (over against the more practical and even anti-Romantic perspective of her father's side) seemed similarly responsive to sunsets, storm clouds, snow-capped peaks, as well as waving fields of grain.

Dad on honeymoon in his newfound heart land.

On three or four occasions I heard my father say he had dreamed of a wide and beautiful land when he was young – and that when he first came to Montana after meeting my mother in Chicago, he found it to be the place of his dreams. That is quite a remarkable thing, however one analyzes it.

My mother's enjoyment of the Big Sky and the world under it seemed to have been informed in part by the literary legacy she had through her mother and her mother's father (a small town western newspaper editor and fantasy novelist, who wrote in the ironic and florid style of Clemens et al). She also profited from the emphasis on memory and rhetoric which was a much larger part of education, especially rural education then than it had become by my day. Until the very end of her life, my mother could reel off fairly large chunks of popular poetic classics. And when I was young, beside the duets she and Dad would sometimes break into (Moon River, Bali Hai, Sentimental Journey, Bicycle built for Two, etc.) we were occasionally treated to spontaneous poetry recitations appropriate to a scene or event opening up before us.

This tradition has been carried down among a few of my generation – I think of my Dyrland cousins – and into the next as well – I think of my cousin's son, Andy Long. Representing my grandmother's generation, Aunt Mimi was also quite a storehouse of verse – I recall especially the delight she took in rendering "The Cremation of Sam McGee," and "The Deacon's Wonderful One-Horse Shay." Grandfather also had a favorite recitation or two. I recall his somewhat wavering voice singing "The Preacher and the Bear".

So deep down and early on it was demonstrated to me both that there was valuable if unobtainable treasure in the human experience of the created world around me, and the possibility that something like that beauty could perhaps be captured in poetry.

My mother had a poet's heart as well as a good memory for poetry, but for reasons which are beyond my assessment, she never applied herself to writing good poetry. She was quite capable of dashing off an amusing set of verses to celebrate someone's birthday, but she had never been placed under the austerity of severe editing or instruction in serious poetic composition. Nevertheless her own efforts and encouragement spurred me to try to write poetry as early as fifth and sixth grades. The artificiality of those early efforts is

135

patent. I don't think I wrote anything that I would defend today until I was 15 or 16, at which point I began to compose "folk song" lyrics that came closer to attaining the standards of a genre than anything I wrote until much later. By my senior year in high school I was writing some lyrics that had a germ of genuine poetry in them.

Backyard photo - First day of school in Fort Benton, 1966.

I'm guessing I was in 7th grade when one of the mothers in a ladies group Mom belonged to – was it Republican Women? – thought it would be amusing to put together a "Beatle's group". The Mersey River gang had swept the country and Beatles clown wigs were for sale in every variety store. So my cousin Howard Hanford, and his classmates Bobby Appleby and Gene Bennett and I (a year younger) were drafted to learn two or three early Beatle songs and perform them for the ladies. I remember we did, "She Loves You," and "If There's Anything That You Want." They loved us.

Performing publicly was a bigger part of small-town life then than it is now – in contrast to urban life. That is to say,

80 percent of us performed publicly in some capacity, albeit only in a chorus or a bit part in a musical.

With cast of "I Remember Momma".

My first "engagement" in a public performance, not counting Sunday School programs and so on, was in sixth grade, when the Senior class asked my teacher, Mrs. Culbertson to recommend someone to play "Arnie" in "I Remember Momma". My mother gave permission, which still surprises me, especially as my lines consisted of "Damn! Damn! Damn it to Hell!" These words were taught me by my uncle in the play (played by Ed Ronish)[8] to be used whenever

---

[8] Ed Ronish graduated as Salutatorian and went on to get degrees in physics from MSU and the University of Michigan. He worked at Goddard Space Flight Center on the Voyager spacecraft, worked in London programming British

the pain of my character's crippled leg was overwhelming. I practiced at home with a wicked feeling as I said these words, especially since I was expressly forbidden to say them anytime outside of the drama itself.

After that the stage ought to have been my oyster-shell, but it wasn't. I always found performing thrilling, but I also hated it. I think I have reconciled those feelings in the last few years. I was in a one act play in 10th grade, and a quartet in "Babes in Toyland." As a senior I was "Woody" in "Finian's Rainbow," which musical is now quite discredited as racist, and which I recall as blasphemous and immoral. But high school students will perform what they are given to perform!

The author as "Woody".

communications satellites, and spent 30 years making digital maps for Honeywell. He died July 23, 2012, aged 70, while playing volleyball.

Nonetheless I feel a certain affection and am grateful to Miss Tesch, our music teacher and director. The experience of stretching my voice to its maximum was very good for me. Incidentally, I fell in love with my best high school sweetheart (Chrissy, a sophomore) during those days of the rehearsals. It was a blissful epoch.

A few months later I recall having the strangest feeling as our class sat robed and mitered in the high school gymnasium watching the formalities unfold before us. It only then began to perk through my oblivious adolescent skull that this was the end of life as I had hitherto known it! Looking around I saw 47 blue-garbed motes about to explode upon the four winds to be carried far, far from each other with little of the existential matrix left that had hitherto bound us together. And these people all composed a large part of my identity up to that moment!

Ten FBHS graduates (1967) with Methodist Rev. Smith.

One more topic that arises in the midst of these reflections is the concept of "happy childhood". While I can cite hundreds of events and incidents that were outwardly happy ones, I do not feel I had a happy childhood. This assessment stands in stark contrast to the feeling of my father and several of my siblings that they had the happiest possible childhoods. Dad's own childhood memoir he titled *Astray In Eden*.

Conforming to the horrible penchant of our age for self-analysis, I have come up with a number of working theories for my less ideal impressions. But I think the best explanations are parallel to Walker Percy's explication of our modern anxieties as laid out in *Lost in the Cosmos: The Last Self-help Book* and also in *Message in a Bottle*. Our prosperity and outward well-being has doubled back on us and made us neurotics. To go into more detail would be a hopelessly boring display of self-absorption.

However, and more entertaining, one of the things memoirs are noted for is blowing the whistle on others for their misdeeds. More than one memoir has gone through legal proceedings because of a tendency to do this. I cannot see any justification for blowing the whistle on anyone unless that person is well-known to have committed crimes and escaped the appropriate prosecution or punishment. It's possible I may mention one such case before this memoir is completed.

However, the one person whom I think we can appropriately blow the whistle on is ourselves, because those of us who claim Christ as Savior cannot very well act as though we didn't have a lot we needed to be saved from. Confessing one's sins in too much detail may be counter-productive, but failing to confess ones sins at all is deceit. Therefore I am dedicating the next couple of pages to confession.

Not all our expeditions and foraging were healthy. On more than one occasion we discovered pornography at the old dump – and I was early and eagerly plunged into adulterous imaginations. There were several episodes where my lust and that of other boys led to various petty larcenies. One friend stole a dirty novel from his parents – and for weeks we secreted it in a dugout in our back lot. One barber shop in town was known for its girly magazines, and when a particularly bold issue was added to the reading material there, several of us scouted it out, then induced a younger member of our cohort to steal it. This he accomplished expertly by rolling it up and putting it in the sleeve of his jacket. However when we went to his house to share in the spoils, we found him sick in bed – sick with guilt, and being such good friends, we attempted to cure his malaise by absconding with the stolen goods. I think that magazine ended up in a cave in the hills before it disappeared.

Another time I am deeply embarrassed to recall, I went to a friend's house and finding his parents weren't home, talked him into ransacking their books in hopes of finding something salacious – unsuccessfully in that case. And yet another time we found a "girly magazine" at the dump and a friend and I stashed it in his cow barn.

Among my parents' own books I found every bedroom scene there was – most of them consisting of two or three sentences, but my imagination didn't need much of a springboard.

What a trove I found back in the storage closet of my Dad's office – a box of US Camera magazines, which every four or five issues, featured a nude photograph. Over a period of time during which I thought I was undetected, I sneaked every issue out and I found every last Venus. Wanting a lasting collection of my own, I traced many of these, and I think it was the telltale indentations from this that gave me away to Dad. In any case, my father learned what I'd been up to and once, very briefly, tried to assure me that these things were not worth obsessing about! Too little and too late.

My obsession with imaginary sex began very early, probably when I was nine or ten. Several cousins contributed to it with dirty jokes, nude displays, and on a couple occasions with more flagrant displays. I also think I had a hyperactive imagination from birth – and this was strong meat for it.

However, I must also say that in retrospect, I am deeply thankful for my uncontrollable lust and addiction to imaginary sex – because it is probably the principle thing that drove me to Christ.

I was a high achiever, a successful student, respected for my musical and later athletic ability. I was known to be intelligent, well-behaved, with a fair sense of humor and not bad looking. As far as outward appearances went, I had everything going for me – BUT inside, I knew myself to be a can of worms. And that's what prepared me to hear and believe the good news that Jesus Christ could help and deliver sinners.

In the trombone section of the FBHS marching band, 1965-66.

At the end of the summer before ninth grade I was visiting a classmate and he and I and a girl from our class ended up telling dirty jokes. This was on the one hand exciting, but on the other convicting to me even then in my confused way, for I realized this was "upping the ante," by involving others in my immorality.

That evening I went over to the football field with several companions, where we amused ourselves by climbing up on the roof of the "Snack Shack" and jumping off. As dusk came on, and I was poised on the edge of the roof ready to jump, I caught my pants cuff on a big nail sticking up and instead of jumping – I dived. My companions clapped and laughed – apparently it was quite a sight. However, the result was that in trying to bring up my hand to soften my landing, I struck full force on the back of my wrist – and snapped it. I also struck full force on the side of my face. It's a wonder I wasn't knocked out. But in response to their laughter, I cursed and held up the obviously broken wrist, demanding to know if they thought that was funny.

After the medicos set the wrist with a plaster cast, and I had a moment to reflect, I attributed that accident to God's discipline for the dirty jokes exchange earlier in the day. I had no theological framework for such a conclusion, nonetheless I was pretty sure of that connection. And would now contextualize it with Hebrews 12 – those the Lord loves he disciplines . . .

Yet like the good Victorian a college tutor once labeled me, I was capable of full scale hypocrisy in regard to sexual morality. At the same time as I was a cesspool of adulterous imaginings, and as I have said, willing to tell dirty jokes in select company, I maintained spotless purity in public. Once Dad took Pete and me along on business of some kind to another farm near town. There while Dad transacted his business a girl about my age showed us around, and in the bunkhouse, hauled out some dirty magazines a hired man had left there. I expressed great disapproval, which was anything but how I really felt about the opportunity to fuel up my imagination. For my public I took the moral high ground, so to speak, although my natural terrain was the swamp. It was a great joy to me to discover in later years that girl came to Christ and has a godly marriage and family.

I wrote a poem a number of years ago in which I memorialized an early incident that long since haunted me with a vague sense of what grace is – what it might mean to be undeservedly forgiven. This must have been when I was about seven. It took place in the Old Methodist church, since very much gone to ruin. It was there my parents were married – I have the photos. And there at least the first four of us kids were baptized –probably in 1957.   (Was Jon, born that year, also baptized there?)

My Robinson cousins had another set of relatives surnamed Birkeland, and one of their great-uncles was Trygve. He was a craggy-faced character with a wonderfully gravelly voice, and as I recall from later on, a gift for story-telling. But on one occasion the church was holding some sort of an event, a pot-luck or something. This had the building pretty much filled up with people coming and going and we youngsters, perhaps having sat through a service for a while already, were full of energy and tearing around the building.

At some point a game of tag or the equivalent must have sprung up because, fleeing as though pursued by vicious foes, I ran out the Franklin Street door, flinging the door open with all my strength and struck Trygve a serious blow in his high Norse forehead. I remember seeing the blood welling up and running down from the wound I had inflicted. I turned and fled certain I had done something unforgiveable and was soon going to have to pay for it. I avoided him all that day. I waited for the phone call, the personal visit, that would land me in hot water, yet it didn't come that day or the next. Nor the next Sunday. Nor ever after. When I finally summoned enough courage to approach the vicinity of my victim, I never received one word of reproach or rebuke. He acted as though it had never happened. That stands in my memory as a powerful parable and he as an icon of Grace, undeserved favor and mercy. As I said, I wrote a poem about it many years later.

MONTANA METHODISTS

The old Methodist church was a frame building with white clapboard siding and an old-fashioned bell tower. The bell was never used in my day, however, being reputed, like the Liberty Bell, to be cracked. Many events and gatherings took place there up to the time the new church building was completed (1957). We held our Vacation Bible School there, and Cub Scout troop 47 met there. It was also the scene of frequent pot-luck dinners, scout and church carnivals, and the like. Both the fellowship hall and the sanctuary seemed huge to me in those days, perhaps because they were often full of active people talking, playing, eating, and singing.

Old Methodist church, scene of many family events.

We were good Methodists – doing everything that was available, Sunday School, (my mother often taught), Vacation Bible School, junior choir, senior choir, singing solos, going to MYF, and Dad served on the church board for a number of years. Under George Ritchey, Bobby's father, I "joined" at age 14, since that was what was being done. I had considerable misgivings because I had gathered enough to know you were supposed to believe something specific to join a church, and I really didn't – but they all assured me that a vague faith in God was sufficient, and mine was sufficiently vague!

Ready for church. Mom & four kids in Easter finery.

In fact, I did firmly believe in God as some sort of superior spiritual power who at least occasionally dabbled in human affairs. I arrived at this level of faith when I was 11 at Kings Hill Methodist Camp near Neihart in the Little Belt Mountains. That old CCC-built camp no longer exists due to the stringencies of the Forest Department, on whose land it was built. Curiously my own children have had the privilege of going regularly to a very similar camp, also CCC built, at Hickory Run State Park in Pennsylvania. I guess the CCC had a basic set of plans they followed in all similar projects.

I attended summer camp there several different years. My first year may have been the previous one, and I can't recall too much except that I talked with an African-American there for the first time in my life. (It was within a year or two that a couple of African-American airmen from Malmstrom Air Force Base came out and played and sang at the Highwood Methodist church which we occasionally attended in the summers. On that occasion Mom and Dad invited the two men back to our farm along with a number of relatives, and although they were also well-fed, the poor guys were practically worn out singing and playing the piano there.)

In these days of renewed racial tension, it is striking to me how firmly we were taught that looking down on others based on how they were made was wrong. No matter how many times we might make a decision by reverting to "eeny-meeny-miny-mo" we never were allowed to catch anything other than "a tiger by the toe." Being Republicans was not just a matter of preferring Eisenhower, Nixon or Goldwater, but of being of the party of Lincoln who freed the slaves. We were taught all men were indeed created equal.

Add to that on my father's side that his grandfather and great-uncles fought with Maine units of the Union Army, where our great-grandfather had been crippled for life (at Petersburg). Nor was there any ambivalence on our part why he had so fought – strengthening the federal government was not our desire nor even preserving the Union. We regarded the Civil War as ending of racial slavery. Regardless of revisionist histories, and despite being nearly an all-white community, these things were important to our family and kin, although, as I've said, we knew some overt racists.

(It is also true that "nigger" was a favorite *sub rosa* insult exchanged among many of the high school boys, but although I knew it was not an option for me (any more than referring to a girl or woman as a sexual object), it seems to me the spirit of those white kids calling other white kids "nigger," was very close to that of the urban black kids I hear using it on other black kids that here in Philadelphia, that is, it was meant to be affectionate and derogatory at the same time.)

The summer I was eleven, my cousin Howard Hanford went with me to Kings Hill, and I'm pretty sure Bob Ritchey was there, too. Among our counselors were a couple of fun-loving Methodist pastors, Joe Loos and George Baldwin. I remember a pastor told us boys a dirty joke the first day, and couldn't understand our ambivalence about laughing at it.

Also at this camp there was a high school girl (a senior?) named Carole Ann, who I grew to like very much in a short time. Having no older sisters of my own, I had no similar older female friends with the possible exception of my cousin Nancy Long. Carole Ann had sisters and friends there, too, in a cabin not far from ours. We had several guys from Great Falls rooming with us. It was a good week – lots of hiking, some volleyball and other sports, wonderful singing around the campfire, where Carole Ann was one of the leaders. In general the week was one of great camaraderie.

The last night of the camp (a Saturday?) we had an evening service in the chapel, and as per Methodist tradition (John Wesley dated his conversion to being "strangely warmed" in a Moravian meeting) there were strong emotions felt by many, especially as the service ended with communion and singing. There were many who "got it" and indeed that expression was used in discussing what happened. Discuss it we did. We boys had gone back and got our PJs on, and talked about it together in our bunks. But a little later a gaggle of the girls came over and sat on our porch, talking with us through the windows. We talked about what "had happened" with practically no vocabulary to describe it.

After half a while, one of Carole Ann's friends fell asleep on the porch, so still "high" on our evening's experience, four or five of us piled out of our bunks, and quite uncharacteristically unselfconscious of our garb, carried the supine young lady back to her cabin, with her friends cheerfully escorting us. We said good night and returned.

I will say here my desire over the next few years was for God to manifest himself in a similar way more regularly – but I was quite frustrated that did not happen. I wrote a simple poem trying to express that "something" in that campground had impacted my heart, but could not give much definition to the "something". In fact the next four or five years continued to be ones of intense spiritual failure so far as I could see.

Still I remained "religious," active in Methodist Youth Fellowship and in the church choir. My junior year I was elected to state MYF office (Stewardship Chairman or something) and my senior year I was elected state vice president. I remember writing an article in our state MYF newsletter asking the question whether the US had a responsibility to protect Southeast Asia from communism, as per Jesus with the money-changers in the temple. I imagine that was the last "conservative" article ever to appear in a Montana Methodist publication.

Although few people who were involved seem to have had the categories to recognize it, the United Methodist Church in the Western Conference (Rocky Mountain Conference) had been co-opted and was selling out to full-blown theological, moral, and political liberalism. In my case, I didn't know because I didn't really know what the Bible said, or what the Christian message was. The fact that church body now has a lesbian bishop is a natural outcome of believing something other than God's word. The only things that came across as sure for us Methodists growing up were you shouldn't drink nor smoke, and you should be nice to people.

Since my father smoked a pipe, it appeared even those rules were flexible. My own tobacco use started fairly early.

I think I was about ten or eleven one spring, -- it must have been a Saturday -- when I went out to the farm with Dad to haul grain to the elevator at Big Sag. The elevator operator at Big Sag was Dewey Burchak, and he was a larger than life character. He and his wife Velma were the only denizens of the metropolis of Big Sag, which in turn took its name from the long, wide u-shaped valley in which it lies, reputed to be the prehistoric bed of the Missouri River during an ice age.

Dewey ran the elevator from the shed-roofed office built up against it. Farmers brought in truckloads of wheat and barley, which they drove into the scale shed, where Dewey weighed the load before and after the farmers dumped the grain in "the pit" beneath the grates of the scale. The grain was tested variously for the amount of trash in it and for protein, etc. Based on these analyses the farmers received more or fewer cents per bushel from the grain companies that owned the elevators – Greeley, General Mills, etc.

Dewey Burchak

Dewey not only ran a grain business from his elevator, but his office was something of a social center for the

Highwood bench and certain strata of the general Highwood/ Big Sag/ Shonkin community. The central social activity was cribbage. On a good day, four or five men would be gathered around a cribbage board while the two players battled it out. I think there was some money involved, but as a youngster I saw little evidence of that.

Dewey was a tobacco chewer. My earliest memories of his place are of the whole environs being decorated with brown pigments, but in latter years he seems to have spit more judiciously, and things were pretty tidy.

On this particular occasion of my accompanying Dad on a grain run to Big Sag, the social club was in abeyance. After we had dumped our load and been weighed again, Dad and Dewey let the dust clear and began their back and forth palaver about weather and politics that was standard fare. As he talked, Dewey hauled a new plug of tobacco out of his pocket and began to unwrap it. Just before he bit off a corner, he happened to look down at me standing next to him and looking on with what must have appeared hungry attention.

He paused and said, "Do you want some?" I looked over at Dad in silent query. "It's up to you," Dad said, "Go ahead if you want to try it." So I did.

Dewey instructed me to bite off a little, but with candy as my paradigm, I bit off quite a lot. "Well," Dewey said, "You got enough there to last you a couple of days." He then took a bite himself, put it back in his pocket, resuming the discussion of what was wrong with the country.

It was probably two or three minutes later that he happened to glance down at me and he said, "You're looking a little green around the gills, maybe that chaw don't agree with you," then he took a second look and noticed there was no bulge in my cheek nor were my jaws working. "You didn't swallow that, did you!" he asked. When I shook my head in confused affirmation (what had I done wrong?) he barked, as he pointed out the door of the bay, "You get on out there!"

Dad led me out of the scale shed to the gravel ramp where in short order I disposed of my last three meals. It happened fast, and it was thorough. One would think such an introductory experience would be discouraging – but the thing was, I liked the flavor. And later that day I asked Dad if I could chew a little of his pipe tobacco.

I became a regular chewer during a few phases of my life, although my stomach has never allowed me to swallow. I especially got to where I'd chew in the evening when I was reading. My youngest daughter recalls hearing the clink of cup on the glass coffee table from downstairs as a comforting sound when she was going to sleep.

Uncle Francis used to have a story about an old sour-dough up in Alaska who chewed tobacco and being by himself most of the time, was pretty relaxed about where he expectorated. (Dad liked that word, and would sometimes ask, "how do you expect-to-rate?") But one day the old-timer was busily making up some sour-dough biscuits for a visiting dignitary, when he realized to his horror that he had just let loose a rich brown stream into the dough. Well, there weren't the makings for another, nor time to borrow, so he went brazenly ahead and when the visitor arrived, he served up cinnamon rolls!

Eventually I found I couldn't keep my chewing moderate. I ended up with a pouch a day loose-tobacco habit. Thus a number of years ago I quit for good. Now maybe once a month, I smoke a pipeful of tobacco – since I don't really like to smoke, I am able to limit it to that. Why do I do it at all? I suppose it's partly to remind myself I'm not holier than the other addicts of this world, many of whom I get a chance to share my hope in Christ with. I have a few glasses of wine occasionally, too, but I "dry out" a month before going to Belize, and don't touch a drop there. The idea of drinking alcoholic beverages in moderation doesn't seem to be a category in that country and I don't want the addicts to use me for an excuse! I've only been "drunk" three times in my life and I know a couple of them were painful experiences for some I love.

Feeling dutiful – perhaps on Memorial Day? ca 1958

My own first case of intoxication happened when I was three or four. My parents, who were both artists, talked several of the others in the Hanford clan into a landscape painting expedition up into the Highwood Mountains. It was a hot summer day, and somewhere along the line as the adults focused on their oil paints and paintings, I grew thirsty. Looking around I saw a tray of clear liquid, and upending it, drank it off. In my memory I think of it as being turpentine. It seems to me that's what it was in the renditions of the story I heard from the adults, but it may have been thinner. In any case when the adults realized what had happened they hastily packed up and rushed everyone back down to the Robinson farm, preparatory to rushing me up to Great Falls or into Fort Benton to seek medical help.

However the grown-ups watching me at the Robinson farm, saw no apparent distress, and in fact saw that I was obviously in a somewhat convivial state of intoxication. Uncle Francis got out his 8mm movie camera and recorded me staggering about, trying to climb on a tricycle and falling off the other side, etc. For a few years this footage was a favorite feature of family home movies, but Aunt Florence, being very soft-hearted, thought it was cruel to allow all that laughter at little Jimmy's expense and she threw the film away. Since I rather enjoyed the film myself, I feel the loss to this day. No further complications seemed to arise. I don't know how bad the effects were on my youthful liver, but I still seem to be getting along all right in that department. Maybe that early exposure has something to do with the fact that I was never very interested in alcohol in junior high or high school, when my friends were out having "beer busts." Rather I was at home cooking up triple x movies in my imagination.

The family dressed for church with Dad's Pierce –Arrow, 1966.

THE COUSINS' FARMS

Robinson's farm, along with the farms of my other relatives, was the setting for many memories. A couple of early ones get mixed up in my mind: a rattlesnake encounter, and the occasion of my intoxication - maybe because the former was also an event that I associate with a somewhat altered state of mind – in this case by fear. We had foregathered at the farmhouse one afternoon for a family feast of some sort, and a number of other kindred were there, including Grandfather and Aunt Mimi.

The last to arrive, in fact, was Uncle Francis Robinson who had been plowing to the west of the farmstead, and arrived on his caterpillar tractor. Dwight, who was just a little younger than I, went out through the tall grass toward the approaching tractor, and I went along with him. Right next to a long galvanized water trough, we came upon a coiled rattlesnake, which with the courtesy of its kind, let us know of its presence, "with bells on" as the British say.

I was absolutely terrified, while Dwight seemed to take it more or less in stride. As I recall, we climbed upon the upside down trough and hollered. Adult help arrived swiftly, no doubt armed with a spade which was the standard weapon for dispatching unwanted reptiles. I remember several other bits and pieces in connection with this. One was that some adult, probably Grandfather went to lengths to reassure me that I was a brave lad and needn't be terrified by rattlesnakes. As I recall, they had cut the poor thing in several pieces, and encouraged me to come close and perhaps even touch one of the pieces, which was no doubt still moving, since snakes, like chickens, do not cease locomotion at their deaths. I was made to feel something of a hero for surviving the ordeal, much in the manner of St. George and the dragon.

Speaking of chickens, nearly all my farm cousins raised them. There was even a while in the early days of Dad's farming that we had a chicken house, but I can't honestly recall it as inhabited. At both Uncle Norris's and Aunt Marian's farms, I had the occasional privilege of helping to feed and water the chickens and gather eggs. I also remember, at age nine or so, being a participant in a morning of butchering chickens at Uncle Norris's.

Cousins and Highwood friends at the Robinson farm.

It was quite remarkable how after Norris whacked the creature's head off with the ax on a wood block, the chicken would take off running – sometimes for a fair distance. I think Howard and I were assigned to chase after them and pick up the reluctantly still bodies by the two feet and carry them wherever the temporary morgue was, before the rest of the process went forward – scalding and plucking and cleaning and singeing, and so on. I don't think I participated in these more advanced activities then, but I remember Aunt Marian teaching me how to pluck and clean a chicken, in the utility sink in their back porch. Her instruction included biology lessons in regard to the different parts of the bird, notably the crop with its collection of pebbles, etc.

Six Trotts and three out of four Dyrlands at their place.

My cousins Dave and Howard Dyrland were close to my age, and were rather intrepid companions. They had one of the biggest barns on the Highwood bench, visible for miles around, and those two would climb high up inside the barn and walk along the narrow planks and even upon the cables that were strung across the chasms of its interior. Once or twice I followed them up in the barn, but that was the extent of my courage. I was utterly certain one of them or both was going to fall to his death right before my eyes, and therefore it was incumbent on me to preserve my life in order to tell the tale. They were my only cousins to keep pigs, and they always had an interesting variety of vehicles about the place.

Uncle Cliff seemed to enjoy the mechanical side of farming and farm maintenance more than the other uncles, and always had a mechanical repair job or two going in his big shop with its homey smells of gas and diesel, oil and grease, with the faintest overlay of sparrow and mouse.

Dyrlands, Howard Hanford, Denny Robinson, Dwight(?) & me.

A famous example of Dave and Howard's intrepidity occurred when they were quite young – perhaps five or six. They went out to play in their overshoes – those black rubber contraptions with the steel buckles up the front which most of us wore in bad weather. Aunt Jean went out to call them in for lunch or something, only to be terrified as she caught sight of them. The two boys had climbed all the way up the fixed ladders built into the far end of the colossal barn, and were walking along the top of the ridge pole in their overshoes – unbuttoned no doubt! As calmly as she was able, she called them to come down. They nonchalantly turned and walked back, descending the ladder – another day, another dollar!

Uncle Cliff, as I have mentioned, also had farmland in the Big Sandy and Boxelder areas. On a few occasions I went with him, the boys and the rest of the family to work and stay in those distant parts. There was at least once I stayed with the whole family in a little trailer – at Boxelder? I recall another occasion when Cliff was hauling grain to one of the Big Sandy elevators, and Dave and I were allowed to buy a bottle of "pop" from the tall cooler in the elevator office. Dave was already knowledgeable as to flavors and recommended Orange Crush, which was like cool nectar to me on that hot dry Montana summer day. Howard's widow, Kay lived many years in Big Sandy, but now lives in Havre. Just a little while ago, her daughter, whose husband is Kenyan, gave birth to a handsome young fellow they have named after Dave.

The other town-farm family in "the Hanford clan" was the Norris Hanfords. My cousin Howard Hanford and I were pretty close, partly because we were the "town" cousins, going to school in Fort Benton where he was one grade ahead of me, but also because I often stayed at their places, both at the farm in the early days, and then in town. The reverse of our progress, they lived in an older house on the farm, but built a new one in town. Howard and I rode our bicycles between farms on several occasions. Spring Coulee in the middle was quite a challenge in those days of single-speed bikes.

Uncle Norris was an innovative farmer, always trying to look ahead to matters of soil conservation, proper fertilizer, and alkali control. He invented many different devices and experimented with new kinds of crop rotation. They had a whole sub-operation going for years which involved planting alfalfa and raising solitary leaf-cutter bees to pollinate it. I think Howard and I always felt a little inferior to our "country" cousins and so we both worked harder to be "cool."

The Robinsons, Uncle Francis and Aunt Florence, occupied what was for a number of years my grandfather's and thus my mother's farm home a few miles from Highwood. Uncle Francis was a wry skeptic and Aunt Florence was a compassionate romantic. There was some degree of

159

dissonance between the two positions. For instance, while Uncle Francis' sense of humor was such that he thought the 8mm footage of my turpentine-drunk worth recording, Aunt Florence's compassion was such that she found it painful to have it shown.

Howard Hanford, Dwight Robinson, Meself, Andy, Pete, Howard Dyrland, Denny Robinson, Dave Dyrland, and Laurie.

Uncle Francis became a health aficionado, reading Rachel Carson and Adele Davis, and he took to having a fairly large bowl of vitamins for breakfast each morning. Aunt Florence and Aunt Marian professed faith in Christ about the same time, and a few years ago Rev. Jim Beadle told me he had no doubt about the genuineness of Florence's faith. But much in the same way that I imagine Grandfather discouraged Grandmother Louise's faith, I think Francis discouraged Florence's. When she developed the cancer that eventually killed her, his response was vitamins, not prayer.

I stayed at the Robinsons often and visited even more. Denny was a little older and Dwight a year younger and we felt sort of "adopted" among their friends on the Highwood bench. As I relate elsewhere, I was allowed to participate in several of their Boy Scout activities as well in many summer activities of the Highwood Methodist church with them and the Longs and the Dyrlands.

Denny half-jokingly says his skepticism about religion dates back to a childhood incident. He got up early one morning while his parents were still in bed and wandered into the kitchen where he climbed up on the counter and looked in the wall cupboards to see what might be worth eating there. He happened on a cupboard that contained various kinds of pills. My impression is that this was before Uncle Francis' vitamin period, and so these were probably genuine pharmaceuticals.

At any rate, when his parents emerged, they found him sucking on a few of these and with many more strewn about, as though he had been sampling them all. They rushed him to Fort Benton where the Catholics ran the St. Clare Hospital. In the emergency room they pumped his stomach. This was not pleasant from Denny's standpoint, and he claims all he remembers is these images dressed in black and white rushing around him and doing things to him he did not like. In his own words, that was his first impression of organized religion.

I got in on a memorable expedition in which the Highwood Boy Scout master, Fred Davison, led a group of scouts, my cousins and friends, on a hike from near the mouth of Belt Creek back up along the creek for ten miles. Through some sort of lapse of consciousness my mother let me go wearing a brand new pair of cowboy boots. I'm sure she, like me, envisioned a nice dry hike along footpaths beside the creek. What we did not know was that the steep walls of the creek canyon with the shifting creek necessitated fifteen or twenty crossings – and the only way to cross the sometimes thirty-foot wide stream was to wade. Furthermore the creek was sometimes chest high with a strong current, and usually had a rough rocky bottom.

All of which meant that though I tried once or twice to take off my boots and carry them high and dry, my feet weren't tough enough to do this, and the boots ended up getting soaked over and over. It was a strenuous hike, even for those with adequate footgear. So pretty early in the hike Fred realized I was the weak link in his band of scouts, and he began to encourage me along. Toward the end, he even lifted me onto the top of his own two feet and held my shoulders, hiking for me, so to speak. We survived it. The boots were ruined. But the chief memory I have is not the misery of it, but the consistent strong kindness of Fred Davison.

At the "White Rocks," sandstone concretions along the Missouri.

I stayed in scouts until I reached Second Class. But Morse code was a requirement for First Class, and it seemed to me an insuperable barrier. I dropped out convinced that I could never learn the code. How petty that seems now!

Most of the expeditions I went on with scouts, family, or friends were more pleasant than that Belt Creek scout hike. My mother and father enjoyed taking the whole family to some of the more scenic spots in Chouteau county – regularly to Lost Lake, up in the Shonkin and Highwood Mountains, down to "White Rocks" along the scenic Missouri from the Big Sandy side, and sometimes just out to the Teton Valley where we puddled around in the river while Dad looked for stones along the gravel-barred banks.

Dad & Mom led us on a painting expedition in the mountains.

We went up into the Shonkins for our Christmas tree most years – sometimes through considerable snow. We had several favorite picnicking spots – one up Kirby Creek, where we often went to hike, to paddle in the stream, or sometimes to fish. More recently I was sitting quietly in the creek there when I saw a creature I didn't even know existed in those parts – a water shrew. It emerged suddenly from a rock ledge on the side and paddled about a bit, then swam back and scrambled down the rock ledge underwater to what I presume was a den below the waterline. Shades of *Wind in the Willows*! On one occasion the whole family set up there for an oil painting expedition, with all eight participating.

A few times we hiked up to the Old Postill Place deeper in the mountains, which has always had a sort of haunting attraction to me.

One of our best babysitters, Mrs. Postill and her husband had settled there, far up in the Shonkin Mountains. There Postill Creek was named for them, and there they raised four daughters and a son. A tragic event occurred, which my mother remembered from her youth. One day the son and a friend, named Eddie Lord, rode bareback down to the town of Shonkin – for mail or groceries or something, and on the way back one of those summer thunder storms rolled in suddenly with a spectacular displays of lightning and thunder.

As they rode, lightning struck them, and both Isaac Postill and the horse were killed. Eddie Lord, however, survived and took the melancholy news to the family. How much longer they lived up in the mountains I don't know. I never met Mr. Postill (also Isaac) but I knew most of the rest of the family, including some grand- and great grand-children.

The old Postill place deep in the Shonkin mountains.

I once took some photographs in the small house which vandals had pretty much trashed over the years. In the photos, dolls and WWI era magazines are juxtaposed among the detritus pack-rats create in any abandoned mountain building. My children have hiked up to the Postill place.

Although in retrospect it seems strange to me, we would often end our occasional trips "to the city" of Great Falls, which were usually for medical or specialized shopping purposes, with some time at Gibson Park. It's only an urban park with little to differentiate it from Fort Benton's own Old Fort Park, except for the big pond in the middle where we could feed the ducks or catch crayfish. I think it may have reminded Dad of his beloved Abbott's Pond back in Andover, about which he sometimes told stories. I think of Gibson Park with warm, fuzzy memories, although it was a far cry from the more exciting wild country we had all around us.

Also a favorite spot for wider family picnics as well as a brief oasis in busy days "in the Falls," was Giant Springs. And oasis indeed it was! Here Lewis and Clark came upon what we were told was the largest fresh-water springs in the United States,[9] pouring out thousand of gallons of clean fresh water per second! Geologists vary on their calculations, but most of them agree the water comes from the Madison limestone aquifer that underlies huge stretches of the Rocky Mountain West, and that much of the water has been flowing hundreds of miles underground for centuries or millenia. A favorite feature of the Giant Springs was a trout hatchery with a big artificial pool full of albino trout. Cliff swallows maintained their mud condominiums on a rocky cliff nearby.

An abandoned homestead was another favorite expeditionary goal from the farm during the summers when we boys had time free to go hiking. This was the old Rice Place down in the Shonkin Creek valley (part of the Big Sag). The history of the Rice family is unknown to me, although I found mention of a Confederate officer Colonel Rice who may

---

[9] A number of springs in Florida seem to have larger outputs.

have been the original homesteader. All the buildings of the place were being used by cattle for shelter, including the at-one-time lovely little cottage/house. It was quite poignant last time I went there with my cousin Ron Long, eight or ten years ago.

Matt and I enjoying Giant Springs.

Dried manure was five or six inches deep through the whole first floor, which had been nicely re-designed, incorporating an original log building, with small rooms, and a bay window facing the barn. The barn was also an impressive structure with a kind of tower in one corner. On an expedition with my brothers and Cousin Dwight when we were young, we once roped a barn owl in the loft of that barn. We then had the dilemma of trying to get the slip knot noose off of the rather snappish raptor. Happily we succeeded and it flew away.

Family expedition to the Old Rice Place on Shonkin Creek.

Although I hunted rabbits and pheasants, and shot a few sparrows , and ground squirrels around the farm, I, along with my siblings, was taught from very young never to kill anything unnecessarily. Rattlesnakes near human habitation were fair game, as were many of the known pests, but we no more would have killed that barn owl than the family dog. In this I am grateful -- my parents were some of the earliest "Greens," without all the Hindu trappings that go with it these days.

I recently was doing some research online and I came upon the Zoophily Society Publication, later called the Starry Cross. These anti-vivisection people made a religion of it, even back in the 1920s, but never achieved our degree of political comedy! Mom and Dad rather looked upon being humanitarian as a natural perspective -- general respect for other creatures.

The first pet I recall, not counting the kitten John Ayers almost traded me for brother Pete, was a kitten named Bootsy. I don't know how we acquired the black cat with white feet (sometime around 1954) but the poor creature did not make it to maturity.

Mom's photo, family expedition to Lost Lake.

As I've said, RJ Culbertson, Bobby's father, and neighbor once removed as well as town postmaster, had a big pen across the back alley from his house where he raised Boxers. Those Boxers were important to him. There were six or seven of them at the population peak, and the reigning queen was a bitch named Kickendorf. All those dogs were energetic and from my standpoint fierce. Bobby would go in the pen to feed and water them, but although I ventured in with him once or twice, I felt anything but safe.

The Boxers ran around the pen and tended to bark in chorus. They occasionally undertook excavation projects, digging under the perimeter wire. One day, the whole pack got out, and charging *en masse* around the block, where they came upon Bootsy, whose education had not prepared her for such exigencies. The event is a blur in memory, but the blur includes a small black ball of fur in the midst of heaving and straining tan backs, all with a grip on the tiny body and all pulling in different directions.

RJ came over later to apologize. Mom met him at the front door and was somewhat more fierce than a Boxer. It was one of the few times I saw RJ looking sheepish.

The assassination of Bootsy took place near the front door of the intervening house, then occupied by the venerable Mrs. Heunig. (Heunig – "hew-knee")

Beyond Culbertsons, lived Mrs. Small who had chicks and gave us cookies. I did not know her grandson, Rocky Highfill, then, although in high school we were to become fast friends. And I've mentioned Mrs. Ayers across the street, who was also kind to us. She and Anna, her "slow" daughter were patient in entertaining us with conversation and snacks.

But between our house and Culbertsons was the small clapboard house that was "Mrs. Heunig's" in my earliest recollections of it. I have only a hazy memory of her. She may have been a bit dotty in her dotage, and I remember the day she died, but I have warm feelings about her. There are a few photo-album images of her in my mind. In one she is holding me up to her kitchen window – over her sink – so I can wave to my mother who is smiling and waving from our house across the side yard. In another (more a short video) Mom and I find a fat cabbage caterpillar in the garden and Mom suggests I go show it to Mrs. Heunig. I knock at Mrs. Heunig's door and she comes out, then with a look of horror on her face, knocks the caterpillar from my hand and squashes it on the worn boards of her small front stoop. I recall a sharp impression of the heavy thick-heeled shoes that did the deed.

Apparently Mom knew full well what sort of reaction I would get – which puzzles me still. There was an almost wanton and childish streak in Mom. As I remember, perhaps partly from incidents like this, Mrs. Heunig got where she didn't trust people very much. She would occasionally accuse someone of something outrageous, as she did Mom one time when she was out weeding the garden. The specifics were not for me. I wonder if she thought Mom was finding more caterpillars to terrorize her with!

The day she died stands out chiefly in the impact it had on other adults. I have an image of Lucille Ulrich, Merlin's mom, sitting in the grass beside their basement apartment entrance and talking with my mother – both of them in quiet and sacred tone about the (then) mysterious circumstances of Mrs. Heunig, apparently of a nature not suitable for children to know about, but rather absolute as to results. I think Merlin's mom had gone to visit her and discovered her body. I also have a fleeting picture of the shining black station wagon pulled up near her door, and a bed with Mrs. Heunig on it being carried between the small pine trees there and slid into the back of the station wagon.

Mrs. Heunig's was the first "death" I directly recall. My grandmother had died when I was 2 ½, but I think I was kept insulated from it to some degree. Mrs. Heunig's death, in the little house right next door, definitely registered on my conscious mind, as I observed the pall of grief in the demeanor and conversation of my mother and Mrs. Ulrich, and others.

After Mrs. Heunig a tall, skinny and smiley fellow name of Vic and his short, curly-haired wife, Hazel moved in to the little house next door.   I think Vic ran the "Time Shop" downtown next to Rudy's shoe shop – or just beyond the Capital Theater on Front Street. There I believe he sold and repaired watches and clocks as well as selling a lot of inexpensive toys, mostly "made in Japan." In those days "made in Japan" meant cheap. Many of the toys were made from tin cans – you could see the print of the original labels on the insides or undersides. What a remarkable thing that in 20 years from the 1950s to the 1970s, "made in Japan" should change so radically to meaning "high quality"!

Then I think Dave Vanhorn, "Shorty" as we always knew him, moved in. He was a bachelor farmer more or less retired. He and occasionally his nephew, "Ronnie" were the denizens of the house during all the rest of my years in school and beyond.   My younger brothers learned how to purloin candy from Shorty, but most of my memories have to do with him dropping in unpredictably every so often, sitting in the sofa in our front room , and in his phlegmatic fashion folding his hands around his protuberant paunch. There he would elaborate on miscellaneous subjects occupying his mind.

Shorty Vanhorn (on right) on Front Street as band marches by.

Sometimes he would fill us in on the doings of Mrs. Panshott, his tenant in the house across the street, a lady who despite the conspicuous lack of a husband, continued to regularly produce more children. This was in the hey-day of the Dependent Child Welfare Act, so of course each child was an additional source of income. Shorty's politics, like my parents', led him to feel there was something profoundly wrong with this, and he might expound upon it.

Another subject which he most often returned to, a kind of hobby of his, was the more spectacular manifestations of religious zeal. He made a point of keeping track what various religious healers were up to, and even studied the behavior of some of the more abstruse sects.

On more than one occasion he saved up to travel down to the Bible Belt and attend a healing service held by Oral Roberts or his competitors. Afterward he would sit on the couch and launch into what seemed the middle of a description of events he had witnessed. Or he might recount the doings of a television preacher recently studied. I recall him telling us about the Doukhobors, a Russian Anabaptist group, many of whom formed communities in Canada around 1900. He told us that when they got fed up with a town or community where they felt they had been badly treated, they would "dust their feet" by taking off all their clothes and go parading naked through the town, never to return again. This intrigued me deeply, and I must admit, still puzzles me.

One time when Shorty was going to be away for a while, he brought over a few items from his refrigerator for Mom to keep for him. I came home from school (high school by then) and found this interesting jar sitting in the fridge. I took it out, removed the lid and took a big whiff – horseradish! I knew nothing about it before, but quickly came to respect it.

It seems to me growing up in the small town of Fort Benton that people were a lot more unique and interesting than modern urban civilization seems to be making us. There were quite a few characters, young and old, with less pressure to conform to some magazine cover or movie-star image. TV had practically no influence – we didn't have one until I was ten. But it is easy to idealize a filtered version of the past. In any case there were characters.

We took an official family summer vacation many years – sometimes just before harvest, sometimes after. My earliest recollection of these was going to Swan Lake in the Swan Valley amidst the Rockies, and then to Seeley and Holland Lakes. Dad loved water – Montana's lack of an ocean was to him (as to John Steinbeck, see *Travels with Charley*) Montana's only shortcoming. Dad loved to row a rowboat, often smoking his pipe as he made his steady but leisurely way on the lake. Sometimes he rented a boat with a motor and I remember at least one afternoon of trolling about the lake with appropriate fishing gear, but catching little. We did catch fish, though, usually off the little docks that went with the cabins we rented.

Mesmerized by the Boob-tube. Laurie had more sense.

Dad hated to borrow. A family that was camping near us at Seeley Lake offered to let us use their motor boat – and I added my pleas to their offer, but Dad refused, telling me you should never borrow anything you weren't ready to pay to replace. While I took that principle to heart for many years, I have come to think there is a kind of charity in accepting such offers as well as in making them. Seeley Lake was also the place where I got the worst sunburn I ever had by wading around in the shallow waters all afternoon attempting to catch sunfish. I only caught the sun – in a kind of double-broiler fashion both directly and reflected from the water. I spent the next couple of days in great pain lying in a tent, where my legs soon shedding huge sheets of skin.

One time at Swan Lake I ended up spending all my waking hours for a couple of days with a slightly older kid whose name I don't know. He kept things lively. We rowed around some in a boat, going up to the end of the lake where a footpath led to a gas station. We tied the boat and walked up to the station where the usual activities were going on.

Swan Lake family vacation, summer 1956.

On the spur of the moment, after watching an attendant apply the removable spout to a can of oil, puncturing the associated hole in the top, my companion took advantage of the attendant's temporary absence to punch holes all around the top of the full can. He then led the way in departing quickly. I was petrified when the voice and footsteps of the attendant rang out behind us along the path. We had just reached the boat when he caught up with us. He then took my companion firmly by the shoulder and marched him back up the path – to what fate I could hardly imagine. But back he came, quite cheerful, saying the customer had thanked him and given him a tip, because that was the wrong kind of oil for his car! I was young, but not so young as to believe that.

Once on one of the earliest lake vacations, Dad showed me a hummingbird nest which he took a long time photographing. On one of those lake vacations I learned to water ski, got up the first time and never fell down, and on several occasions I fell in love for a few days. Once when the whole family rowed across Swan Lake for a picnic, we found the old Klaxon horn which ended up on our model T truck.

The official photo of the hummingbird nest, Mom and kids.

One time at Holland Lake I swam across an arm of the lake – the first time I had ventured that far over deep water. Both my parents were avid swimmers and taught us both on these vacations and in the farm reservoir. In addition to this I went all one winter with the Fort Benton Boy Scouts to the Natatorium in Great Falls. I chiefly remember that place for the certainty I would probably end up drowning there, amidst the unique echo of the tiled pool, and the strong smell of chlorine. Afterwards, however, we would always go to Sandy's Restaurant (later Zandy's) which was perennially picketed by union food workers, but where you could get the

"Businessman's Lunch," a double burger, French fries, and a milkshake, for 50 cents!

Cousin Dwight and I on one of many canoe trips.

Starting about 1963, Tom Leinart and I, and in subsequent summers, cousins Dwight Robinson and Dave Dyrland, and Pete, and various other friends and relatives made canoe trips down the Missouri from either Fort Benton or Carter for as many as four days, usually ending up at the Lohse Ferry crossing. One of the trips was just before Cousin Dave went in the army, and friend Rocky into the marines. Later Roseann and I went on a number of day trips and a few overnight ones down the Missouri.

It was always quite an adventure with the rugged and relatively untouched beauty of the river canyon with its many remarkable rock formations, with a lot of wildlife, and with the hard work of paddling our canoes, often against the wind on a bendy river that sooner or later flows in all four directions. When I was in the Army, Dad and Mom took a leisurely trip just the two of them, as photographs testify.

Mom and Dad on their own canoe trip mid-70s.

A family wide vacation took place around 1957/8. The uncles and the aunts loaded the whole tribe up and we went to Flathead Lake where we stayed in some cabins back up the hills from the lake. Our purpose was not water sports, but huckleberrying. We all went out every day for several days, and brought back gallon upon gallon of huckleberries. With what seems to me (from the standpoint of my family genes) downright wastrel largesse, the aunts cooked up pie after pie and we ate them until we could eat no more. Many coolers full of berries went home with us to be made into jelly and syrup, or to be packed away in freezers for winter pancakes. It was a very successful expedition, although we youngsters probably ate more than we picked. In retrospect I'm a little surprised it didn't become a family tradition, but farming demands conformity to the crops and weather, so that very few regular things can be planned during the seasonable months. Vacations were usually spur of the moment.

Sometime about 1959 or 60, Grandfather organized an expedition to Glacier Park, in fact I think he organized two in a row – one for the boys and one for the girls. There was a rambunctious cohort of us from 9-13 on the boys' trip and as I recall only two or three other adults. We did a lot of day hikes, and saw a water ouzel nest under a waterfall. Sometime early on we formed sides for what at a few points was nearly a civil war rivalry. I think Dwight and I ended up mad at each other for a couple of days.

Hole-in-the-Wall, one of many spectacles along the Missouri.

Factions among the cousins on that Glacier Park trip were nothing new. The tendency among us kids to form rival groups was irrepressible. I recall two "gangs" out at the Robinson farm, chasing each other around and throwing rocks. And in town, using our back lot which Dad later too-kindly gave to the high school for a parking lot, we had various factions and various wars, often digging trenches and even putting roofs over them at our most ambitious.

In keeping with the tradition that you fight with your best friends, I used to have clod wars (clods -dried chunks of mud or sod) with Kent Aznoe – he of rocket fame – and one day in what he thought was a stroke of genius, he went home and got a football helmet, which he put on before commencing to heave clods. Not to be outdone, I began to aim for his helmet, and after a while was surprised and a little penitent after I hit him in the head just below the front rim. He went home mad, but we were soon fast friends again.

Cousins with Grandfather at Glacier.

In about the third year we were at the farm, Aunt Dorothy Partridge brought my eastern cousin David (I had a cousin David on each side of the family) to stay part of the summer with us. I think she was trying to get him away from less than ideal companions, but that's only a vague inference. He helped Dad on the farm, and so I felt a little "bumped down," but despite considerable need for adjustment on his part to our large family, he got on well with his household full of cousins. At the end of that summer we took a trip to Glacier National Park with Dor, Dave, Grandfather and Aunt Mimi, and the rest of our immediate crew.

I remember staying at the Many Glacier Hotel, and eating in the dining hall one night. The waitress (they were mostly college kids there in the summer) took a liking to Dave, but our meal took an interminably long time coming. When

Dad inquired of the waitress she explained that "The cook is in a schnit." Another entry in the family book of apothegms.

I believe it was also on that occasion that as we departed the hotel our last morning there, Grandfather kept hinting to Dad that he ought to tip the room-service maid a little more. They finally reached what looked like an agreeable stipend, leaving it on the dresser there. But as they were departing the lobby, Grandfather turned to Dad with his characteristic streak of mischief and said, "You gave her too much, you boob!"

Now that I think of it, my mother didn't fall far from the tree! I recall her complaining about the time on a trip to the coast with her parents they came upon a fisherman with a basket of fresh oysters, who offered some to these inland visitors. Grandfather urged Mom to try some, "Go ahead Lucille, they say they are very healthy." So Mom choked down an oyster or two and suggested her father follow suit. "Oh, no," he said, "I couldn't eat those things!"

A famous event which took place on the last leg of a return trip from a vacation must go down in the annals of the family. It was an instance of my mother getting the better of my father in repartee.

This took place on the return trip from one of our lake vacations, or possibly a longer trip out of state. In any case, we stopped for lunch on the last day. We were all weary, and Dad was his usual outgoing restaurant humorist, joking with the waitress, at the same time as he and Mom tried to oversee the orders of six not-always-sensible kids. As I recall there were a lot of hamburgers, fries, and milkshakes ordered. At the end of the meal according to ancient tradition which seems to persist in my sons' families, Papa batted clean-up. Half-burgers, remaining fries, and last third milkshakes had to be disposed of. Otherwise they would be "wasted".

Mom tried to persuade Dad that this wasn't necessary. Dad munched manfully on, and no doubt asked the waitress for an air-sick bag. Mom was becoming increasingly uncomfortable emotionally and socially as Dad was obviously becoming digestively and physically. She became a little insistent, and said something to the effect (she had an injured tone she used on such occasions) "Jim, this is getting ridiculous," to which he replied (he adopted a mocking and somewhat lofty tone) "Oh, you're so above me!" -- to which she replied without nary a pause – "Well considering your condition right now, I would rather be above you than below you."

Dad was helpless before a good joke – if he hadn't been on his way to helpless anyway – and he began to laugh and hold his stomach. He stumbled up from the table, went to the door, laughing uncontrollably, and leaned on the frame. Then he staggered on out to the parking lot, where we could see him heaving with laughter as he leaned against our two-tone blue Ford station wagon.

I think I may safely say we kids were all deeply concerned. We were afraid this might prove fatal or at least seriously injurious to him. But he recovered in time, and we drove on home not entirely sure what to think of our parents.

One summer (1963) we arrived home from vacation at one of the lakes, only to find the area had been devastated by a storm the day before. I believe that was the biggest summer storm of my boyhood days, but I don't remember much detail. The summer of 1970, on June 27, to be exact, there was another big storm, and I wrote a description of that one. And since I have done so before, I may have combined details of the two storms in my account. Nonetheless I give it again here.

The storm came in the late afternoon with ominous clouds both in the east and the northwest. We usually get our weather from the southwest, however, so that's where we looked, and after a bit, we could see there was lots of rain coming down in that direction. The day had been pretty warm and still, and we were in need of a little rain. As the storm got closer, we could see the storm line in the clouds. There was a definite line where the storm front was coming against the other clouds, then a couple of miles off in the southeast, we could see the dust line where the storm was approaching across the fields.

I was out trying to take photos, none of which were very good– one can't get that kind of thing on film. Anyway, I was out taking photos when the storm got within a mile of us. It was already noisy, and dust was sailing very high in the air. As it got even closer it seemed as if the dust clouds were circling like a tornado. I retreated into the farmhouse and as I got through the door, I could hear it roaring.

Because it looked and sounded so dangerous, we all retreated to the basement, but we emerged again soon after to watch the rain driven before the 80 to 100 MPH wind. The house shook with the pounding of the gusts. This lasted two hours. After about forty minutes, we looked over toward the little reservoir and there was something new on its far bank. Through the rain we couldn't make out what it was for sure. Then someone thought to look down toward the end of the line of bins, where the old shack was – or rather where it had been that morning. It was gone – picked up and smashed across the reservoir!

The other old building across the coulee – remains of the old Knudson farmstead -- was also blown completely flat. We could not even see the remains from the house. We worried about the steel bins which were directly upwind of the house. The previous year during a lesser storm, one of the roofs tore loose and flew half way across the yard, falling short of the house, by the grace of God. The bins seemed to be holding up pretty well through the first half of this storm, however.

Dad was keeping an eye on the bins when all of a sudden, the roof of one began to ripple along the eaves in a sort of a wave motion that began on the side facing us, but gradually increased until it extended all the way around the roof. What had been going on was the initial lift had broken a few bolts, and then it systematically broke the rest of them loose. Then the near side lifted up like a poke bonnet, but miraculously did not blow off. Some of the bolts or straps must have held. It stayed there all during the rest of the storm, bucking up and down in the wind.

We found out afterward that the far half had sort of blown down into the bin and the angle iron of the door frame had remained secured. That was probably the only thing that kept that huge metal discus from flying across and into the house.

The Longs were outside barbecuing when the storm came up suddenly. Ron looked over toward Highwood Baldy and remarked that it was raining over there. Five minutes later the storm was at their place. They ran inside and they looked out to see the wind starting to pick up coals from the barbecue and rolling them through the dry grass, where they started little fires. Uncle Burton and Ron went to get some water from the tap, but the electricity was already out, so the pump wouldn't run.

Uncle Burton ran out to the garage to get the dog bucket, and as he leaned down to pick it up, something tapped him hard on the shoulder. He looked up and there was nothing there, but suddenly the garage leaned over again, and he had to jump back to avoid it tapping him again. He grabbed the water and put out the little fires. Ron says he went out the next morning and he couldn't even shake the garage!

The Dyrlands had a roof blown off the dormer of their farmhouse, and lots of water got in and did some damage. Apparently over the town of Highwood and surrounding areas there was a lot more rain, someone said two inches. We only had a little compared to that, and there was a great area northeast of the house where the rain didn't hit at all, due to the house shielding it in relation to the driving wind.

The Robinsons apparently had the worst damage of any of the relatives. Their big wooden bin lost its roof. Two of the campers, for which Uncle Francis was a dealer in those days, took off and flew, the one about eighty feet, doing considerable damage to themselves. Their greenhouse lost its west wall, broken into a million pieces which scratched the paint on their car. Dwight said he found glass not only around the corner of the house, but down by the bunkhouse, seventy-five feet or so away.

Photo of loose bin roof seen from the farmhouse during storm.

In Highwood a couple of barns were levelled – and one just had the north wall blown out of it. The huge annex to the Greeley elevator had its roof broken up and the walls caved outward. Much of the roof was blown off the depot, as well. Southeast of Highwood, the wind was so strong it was able to move heavy equipment such as seed-drills around. Several miles of electric line were down east of Highwood.

In Fort Benton, the city shop and the golf course club house were literally blown into a thousand fragments. The city shop blew over into a neighboring home and did thousands of dollars' worth of damage. There were tree limbs up to a foot in diameter snapped off and broken down all over town. We hauled away six big loads from our yard in our pickup. The two blocks of the park were piled high with leaves and branches and logs. Even big pine trees were snapped off.

Pete swimming in the snow! June 13th.

Drew also enjoying the opportunity to swim in the snow!

To the east of town, trailers were blown over. There was bad hail damage in the Great Falls area.

The previous year we had snow on June 13th. The temperature had been steadily dropping for three days under a rain front, and it dipped below freezing for a few hours, during which we accumulated about four inches of snow. It came down the kids' slide due to the warm air temperature and curled into a "Christmas Candy' many layered roll at the bottom! We went down and swam in the little reservoir during the time it was snowing and Dad took some photos of us! During such times Dad liked to sing, a few lines from the state song, "Montana, Montana, your skies are always blue."

Extremes of weather and temperature went with the territory. The thermometer would frequently go above 100 degrees at the peak of summer – although unlike other climates I have been in, it was still quite a bit cooler in the shade at such times.

On the other end, 40 below zero was commonly achieved at some point in the dead of winter. I recall going out coyote hunting with cousins Ron and Dwight when the thermometer was close to that mark, and we were out for two hours or so. The trick was in bundling up with proper layers and keeping head, hands and feet from setting up solid.

And again on the other hand, (the third hand?) we had the regular feature of the "chinook," a warm wind said to originate with the Japanese current in the Pacific which would make its way over or through the mountains and turn freezing winter into a mini-spring often for several weeks, even in mid-winter. Sixty-degree temperatures would prevail during these periods. Then outdoor activities give us a relief from "cabin fever," as the old-timers called the winter doldrums. Chinooks might end quickly, however, and winter revert to its proper freezing nature until true spring gradually made itself felt. In town, the first major sign of spring was the "river going out," which meant that the thick layer of ice that had formed on its surface would break up and cause quite a spectacular ruction, piling up and grinding away at anything near its banks. Many of the town's citizens would engage in lotteries based on predictions of when the river would "go out."

FARM HANDS

When I was eleven, toward the end of the summer, Dad took me out for a couple rounds on the old tractor he'd restored, an International (McCormick-Deering) WD9. We went around a little field near the house a time or two, then he turned it over to me and climbed off. I was deeply proud to join the farming fraternity, and avoided any great mishaps until he came out and took over to finish off the corners. Thirty years later I found a grooved Indian "pestle" while looking for agates in that same field.

Early exposure – on WD9 with Dad.

The next summer I not only drove the WD9, but was turned loose with the bigger Minneapolis Moline, and aside from getting stuck in mud holes once or twice, was on my way to being a professional. Tractor driving had many dimensions.

I delighted in company for it seemed the most solitary of occupations. It was a great treat to have a little brother or sister along for a round or two of the field. The most regular companion was our dog, Bart, who loved vehicular locomotion of any sort, as no other being could. Bart was a faithful companion and seldom began a day that he did not finish. When Bart was not riding, he was trotting along beside the tractor – in the end, that's how he lost his life.

Harvest crew 1961, my first year driving truck

When neither Bart nor a sibling were available, there were other occasional accompaniments, such as the jack rabbit that tried to keep a loose occupation of his territory as the plow changed the face of it. I suppose I spent hours looking for birds' nests and moving them from in front of the plow when I found them. Meadowlarks, lark sparrows, killdeer, and horned larks, with a rare curlew or duck or hawk might inhabit stubble or summer fallow. Redwing blackbirds lived in the marshes and reservoirs near many of the fields. Hawks and seagulls brought home the lessons of nature red in tooth and claw as they followed the tractor feeding on such mice or other small creatures which fled homeless from the plow. The stooping of a hawk never ceased to send a thrill or chill down one's spine.

Driving combine, wheat harvest, 1966

I especially longed for my friends when I drove tractor. I thought of my romantic idols, and dreamed of singing with Bob Dylan – companions I only had in imagination.

In some particular way, driving tractor made one intimate with the land and weather. I learned the mountains and the hills, not only their profiles, but something of their essence. I learned the clouds and the storms. I learned the unrelenting sun and the taste of dust – and I learned to see through it like a superhero with x-ray vision. I learned the smell of rain half an hour before it came. I learned to unhitch the duckfoot and head for home when the thunderclouds rolled in from the southwest. I learned to set my eyes five miles away as well as fifteen feet away. I learned there was no buccaneer like a farmboy on a tractor.

That fall, when I was twelve, I drove truck, and I didn't fare quite so well, what with the various exigencies of backing up to unload in the auger, running the auger without plugging it, and getting to the combine at the proper time and locating the truck under the unloading spout. That year I'm not sure Dad let me unload on the move, which is standard practice for accomplished drivers. I do know I turned too widely on one occasion and dented the right fender of the GMC truck on the lower corner of the combine platform/gas tank. I recall being berated, but no more than I deserved.

I'm not sure if it was that summer or the next that I made one of the more shameful errors truck drivers can make. I had gotten fast enough at my tasks that I usually arrived back in the fields with fifteen or twenty minutes to spare. So I had taken a book along to read – I believe it was *Gulliver's Travels*. Deeply involved with the Brobdingnagians or the Lilliputians, I was shocked when suddenly the truck door flew open and a hand reached in and yanked me out onto the stubble. Dad had a full tank of grain on the far side of the field and had been trying to signal me for fifteen minutes, when he finally got off the combine and walked across to do the job himself!

Those without farm experience may feel this was harsh – however, especially with grain, it begins "shattering out" onto the ground as soon as it is ripe, and so every minute lost is not only lost time for the other harvesters, but also lost grain. I was profoundly chagrined, and wondered if I was fired permanently. However, after unloading the combine, he continued cutting, and left the truck there for me to walk around and recover.

For years I had a Don Greytak pencil drawing on my bedroom wall, which Dad gave me long afterward. It shows a young farmboy sitting in the cab of his grain truck reading a comic book by which he is greatly amused as in the distance the combine driver stands atop his machine frantically waving both arms. Apparently I wasn't the only truck driver to make this mistake!

190

The next year I drove the combine quite a bit, and Pete began to drive truck. By the time Ardy was 11 or 12, Dad had quite a crew of hired men. Doing the work of operating equipment and helping Dad repair it was not only rewarding in that it was "man's work," but it took me away from the "women's work" that had been the lot of we three older boys – that is daily cleaning and (every other day?) mopping our various assigned areas of the farm house. (Did we also do our own laundry?)

Driving combine, harvest 1963.

In a number of other ways I was my mother's oldest daughter until Laurie was 7 or 8. The positive side of this was Mom taught me to bake a whole range of cookies, and in general how to follow a recipe. And I did learn to sweep and mop and wash dishes and clothes – all valuable skills for anyone. But I was mighty glad to get free of these household tasks and do farmwork – at least for the first couple of years.

Our closest farm neighbors were the Don Knudsons. Don, known as "Skid," was a very quiet fellow. Sometimes he would drop over to borrow a piece of equipment, which was how the farm community operated. Dad might borrow a moisture-tester from Skid or a grain-sample probe from Uncle Burton, or vice versa. But when Skid came by to borrow something, it took him half an hour or so to get around to saying what it was. He was also pretty patient, even though some among my brothers, who worked for him a while, tested the limits of that patience.

When we moved on to the farm Don and Evanita were there with three daughters, Donna, Diane and Doreen. Diane or "Tudy," was my age, and later became a classmate in Fort Benton. At that time the older two girls, at least, were still attending the one room Lower Shonkin School, together with Drapers and Grossmans.

The oldest cousins in each of the four farm families: Denny Robinson, Howard Dyrland, Ron Long, and Howard Hanford.

Almost the same distance, but in the other direction were our next closest neighbors, the Glascocks. Bud and Myrtle Glascock had a son who was grown and gone by the time we got there, and another son several years older than me, Gale, known affectionately as "Windy." Dad claimed

Windy had started driving tractor so early that he had to climb down off the tractor seat in order to push the clutch pedal. It was from Bud Glascock that Dad got the model T truck first worked on by Sandy Gibson, and then by Dad and last by me. Mrs. Myrtle Glascock was a lively lady. Among her claims to fame was her ability to de-scent skunks so they were less risky as pets. Although I never witnessed the surgery, my imagination always paled at what that might involve.

For a few years there was another neighbor about a mile away on a farmstead that had its own well – with terrible tasting sulfurous water. The family there in our early days at the farm were the Kellers, the *pater familias* of which was Virgil, who was famous for one of those memorable expressions. He used to drive truck for Dad during harvest in the early days, and when we kids got in his way or became "too familiar" as the expression went, he would threaten to "tear off your leg and beat you with the bloody end of it!"

Combine unloading "on the go" with Pete as truck driver.

I did not know the names of the people involved until a brother told me, but it turns out Virgil was an only child and his parents were the couple we were told about who froze to death a short distance from their own front door. Their story was often used to warn us against taking risks in travelling in winter weather.

The Knudson girls & their cousins Cliff and Larry, summer 1959.

In early March 1944, Cleo and Irene Keller drove home from Great Falls where both of them had spent several days undergoing medical treatment, since both were in poor health. They started out the middle of the afternoon, passing through Fort Benton, and eight miles later noticed they were low on gas, so they stopped at the Guy Bramlette ranch (the very place Roseann and I stopped for gas on a cold winter night 28 years later) where they got five gallons before proceeding on their way.

They travelled the Shonkin Road then turned off (on what we called the Black Butte road) going another mile or so when they developed engine trouble of some sort. This was witnessed by Ira Behimer, whose ranch they had passed a little before they stopped and lifted the hood to work on the car for quite a while. Cousin Ron recalls that the Behimers invited them to stay there, but giving up on the car, they instead set out about 7:00 PM to walk the two miles remaining of their journey home. There was a lot of snow on the ground and the wind was blowing hard.

Diane and Doreen Knudson let us ride their horse and pony.

They were greatly hampered by the snow, the wind, and their own weakened conditions. Ron recalls there was evidence they sought temporary shelter in a cattle shed, where apparently they tried to start a fire but found the straw too wet to burn. So they struggled on until about 150 yards from home, the two of them came to a halt. Perhaps she said she couldn't go on and he stopped with her – or vice versa. In any case the next morning her brother, Jay Emmens, who had been staying at the ranch, went out to feed cattle and found them. Virgil was serving in the army, first in Africa, and at the time of the accident, in England. After he got out of the army, he took over the farm.

One time a bunch of the younger kids went with mom to the Keller's for some fresh chicken. It was the first time some of the younger ones had seen chicken butchering. Matt says it was quite traumatic, and he still has vivid recollections, perhaps somewhat improved by imagination. Mrs. Keller held chicken by the feet in one hand, and laid them on a block, where she whacked off their heads. She released each one, and they took off running or flying in various directions. Matt swears a couple of them flew up and lit on the roof of the coop – he can picture one without a head landing next to one that still had its head, and the awkwardness of conversation between them.

Virgil had a daughter who was about Pete's age. One time we had such a successful harvest that we had nowhere to store all the grain and Dad ended up filling up the back end of the Quonset with wheat. One day late in the summer, the Kellers were visiting. When it came time to leave, eight-year-old Pete and the daughter were not immediately to be found, but were located out in the Quonset, swimming in the grain, and having a great time.

The family moved to Fort Benton a couple years later and one day the daughter stepped on a honeybee that stung her and she had such a terrible reaction that she stopped breathing within a couple minutes. By the grace of God, they were only half a block from the only hospital within forty miles, and they gave her several injections of atropine or adrenaline, or whatever it is they give such persons, and she recovered fully.

For most of our years the Henry Grossmans were our third closest farm neighbors – about two miles away, while Knudsons were only ¾ of a mile away. The two boys Tim and Ron were close to the ages of me and Pete, but we didn't see a lot of each other.

The Knudsons became closer friends, particularly because most summers their cousins, Cliff and Larry, came to stay with them, or with Grandma and Grandpa Knudson, and they were just the same age as me and Pete. We spent countless hours going around the big reservoir and catching whatever critturs offered to show their faces, often with the Knudson girls or their cousins joining us. The Knudsons also had horses, and I pretty much learned to ride from them.

Drew and I on the Knudson's horses.

Skid was an expert welder – later in life he became pretty close to blind, largely as a result of too many welding flashes. He was also quite a mechanic. He built a wonderful little belt-driven car with an auger motor for the kids to drive around, and we felt greatly privileged when they would drive it over and let us ride with them. (Much later my brother-in-law Ed acquired the car and my nephew Kirill/Danny spent countless hours alternately crashing it and tinkering with it.)

The rural phone system was set up entirely on a "party line" basis, which means that you shared a line with perhaps ten or twelve other families. Each had a distinct phone number and a distinct "ring," so that, for instance if the phone rang two longs and a short (more or less equivalent to Morse code two dashes and a dot) you knew that someone was calling the Drapers, or if it rang three shorts, you knew it was the Zantos – that sort of an arrangement. However, no matter who was called or who was on the line, anybody could pick up the phone and listen in. That way if there was an emergency –

197

say a fire near by, everybody could find out quickly. On the other hand, privacy was harder to come by.

Diane "Tudy" Knudson, farm neighbor,
friend & classmate.

When we first moved to the farm, the Knudsons and Drapers were particularly glad to have some new victims for their phone pranks! They would call up and ask such questions as "Is your refrigerator running?" To which you were obliged to answer, "Why yes it is," to which they would gleefully reply, "Well, then, you better go and catch it!" Alternatively they might call and ask, (quite appropriately as it turned out, since Dad was a pipe smoker,) "Do you have Sir Walter Raleigh in the can?" To which one was again obliged to answer in the affirmative, the response invariably being, "Well, you'd better let him out!" Other such telephonic riddles enlivened our tranquil hours, always ending in abundant girlish giggles, usually in gaggles.

Both Knudsons and Glascocks ended up divorced, and the community judgment was that the two ladies, who were close friends, had been bad for each other. On these first occasions of seeing the devastation of divorce, our family shared some of the pain although we expressed it mainly through our awkwardness. We remained close friends, and I feel privileged that Tudy and her husband Jim Moore continue to be our friends as well as fellow believers in Jesus.

Another mile and half north beyond the Knudsons in the Shonkin Creek valley lived another family with kids our age, the Kurths. Their aunt and uncle, Mabel Evers and Jock Watson, lived near the town of Shonkin proper, which consisted of a depot, an elevator, and a combined store and post office. The Watsons and Kurths were active in Farm Bureau and/or the Republican party with my folks. One time my mother and brothers were down at the Watson's for a gathering and the kids were running through the barns, when one of them, Robin Marcuson, got kicked by a horse. He recovered fully, but I recall lectures followed that event!

Another Trott Family saying arose from the fact that Dick Kurth pastured his cattle near us, and the fences weren't all they should have been. One time Dad called Dick to tell him his cows were in our barley and not improving its chances any. Dick replied cheerfully, "Them's yearlin's for ya!" in exactly the tone appropriate for "boys will be boys!"

The earliest memory I have of the Kurths was at their place in the mountains when I was only five or six. We were invited to a Fourth of July celebration at their ranch, where Dad and Dick and possibly Herb Pasha were outdoing one another setting off fireworks. They started putting firecrackers under tin cans to see who could fire them highest in the air. Somebody put a couple of firecrackers under a can and it just about set the record for height – however unbeknownst to the artilleryman, the lid of the can had been in the bottom and the explosion shook it loose toward the top of its trajectory, so the lid came slicing down through the air and struck an older gentleman in the cheek. [10] He had quite a gash and was bleeding profusely. This radically changed the atmosphere. The fireworks came abruptly to an end as some administered first aid then took the injured man to town for stitches.

On another occasion, the summer of 1966, right after school was out, Jim Herbold and I went up into the Shonkin mountains on a fishing trip. We went way up Kirby creek, and as I did all too often, I drove where I shouldn't have. In fact I was being too smart for my own good, because I knew a bend in the road near the creek was very muddy, so I tried to cut off across a grassy stretch and avoid the mud. In fact the source of the moisture was a spring in the middle of that grassy stretch – and I got us stuck, but good.

Jim Herbold, friend and classmate.

---

[10] Matt recalls Dad telling the story with a different twist – that the damage was done by a can that had been previously in a fire and thus came unsoldered at the seam with the explosion, flattening out and slicing through the air and the face.

All the four-wheel drive could do was dig us deeper in! After thoroughly convincing ourselves of this fact for three hours or so, all the time stuffing boards and branches and rocks under the spinning wheels, I told Jim we would have to hike back down the road to Kurth's, hoping someone was home who could bring a four-wheel vehicle up and extricate us. It was a scenic hike, and took us probably 45 minutes.

We got to Kurth's about dusk and as Jim went in to check if anyone was home there, I ran on down toward where we'd seen a few campers earlier that afternoon. A quarter mile later, I became aware that I was being followed, and as I got off the road and turned around, there was Dick and Jim riding along behind me greatly amused at my exertions. Dick then drove his pickup back and using a chain, pulled us right out. We retired a respectful distance from the mudhole and camped.

Probably two years later, Jim and I were both invited to a party at the Kurth's new house in Fort Benton. At some point in the party, Dick and his son, Doug, entered on a long narrative about two campers who had gotten in a much bigger jam than we had up in the Shonkins.

It seems these two greenhorns had driven into something equivalent to a beaver dam high in the Shonkins, where they had all but sunk their vehicle, and after wallowing in mud up to their necks, had walked down the road in the middle of the night to awaken the whole Kurth household with their tale of woe. Samaritans that they were, both the older male Kurths had got out the caterpillar tractor and made the long and tedious trip far into the mountains where using a logging chain which nearly broke in the process, they had extracted the vehicle after much misery and swearing.

Both Jim and I marveled that someone could have made so much worse a mess of it than we had, but Dick and Doug both swore that in fact WE were the persons in this story. Not only did Jim and I marvel we had forgotten so much of the story's true drama, but that day had become night, a pickup had become a caterpillar and Dick in the singular had transmuted into Dick and Doug in the plural!

After I was married and gone, the Kurths got themselves into deep trouble with the law which resulted in jail time and the loss of their ranch. They rigged up a large marijuana-growing enterprise in the second floor of a farm building, hidden by a false ceiling, as well as a set-up to extract hash oil. Through some sort of conflict with a couple of drug-buying middlemen, the law got on to their operation.

Rocky and Jill Highfill at their ranch at Shonkin.

Dick was later interviewed on the nationally televised Today show, talking about the plight of the American farmer and how a fellow might get driven to doing things against his better judgment in the effort to make ends meet – but there wasn't much local sympathy for that argument. However from what I am told, I think it was another case of the Lord using the hard things they went through to lead a number of the family to Christ.

The Draper family lived down in the Shonkin valley at the foot of the mountains west of Shonkin town. Johnny Draper was from Maine, a Yankee like Dad, and I think they had kindred feeling about that. "Beatty" Draper and Mom got along well. They had four lovely daughters, and once in a while we got to bask in their beauty. I once went out riding with a couple of them, probably Connie and Pam, and the lively horse I was riding stopped abruptly as I went flying over its head into a patch of thistles. Horsemanship rated high as a masculine skill – and I knew that all my romantic hopes had just died! Wanda Draper became a good friend of Patty Culbertson, so I saw her occasionally at Culbertson's in Fort Benton. Connie became an important administrator in Fort Benton, much in evidence as an organizer and manager of the summer parade and Art in the Park in more recent years.

Jill Draper married another of my best friends, Rocky Highfill, a high school classmate and Highwood farm neighbor of my Dyrland cousins. They ended up on the Draper ranch, where Roseann and I often visit, Jill becoming one of Roseann's best Montana friends.

Rocky Highfill and I, perhaps because we both had one foot on the Highwood bench and the other in Fort Benton, became close buddies. This despite the fact that he had a tendency to plague me in minor ways. For instance, one time he and I spent most of an afternoon trying to catch one of his horses out in his Grandfather Small's pasture, which was pretty frustrating, because every time we got the critter cornered, the horse kept outsmarting us. But at one point I found a stick of gum in my pocket and proceeded to chew it.

When Rocky saw I was chewing gum he asked me why I didn't give him any, and when I aid it was my only stick, he asked why I didn't give him half. I said I was sorry but I didn't think of that. He said why didn't I give him half now. Thinking he just might be enough of a character to actually my half-chewed gum, I pulled off a piece and offered it to him, at which point he threw it away, laughing at my gullibility.

He used to eat raw eggs, and when he found out I found this somewhat repulsive, he decided to get some mileage out of it. So one day after lunch, he walked back the five blocks to the high school, where in the ten minutes before classes started, he chased me up and down the halls trying to get me to look at the raw egg he had held in his mouth all that time purely for the pleasure (?) the displeasure to me would give him. Yet we're still buddies!

In the early days on the farm when we had cousins staying over or were otherwise ambitiously inspired, we would hike or bike down to Shonkin town and the only emporium within 15 miles, that is "the Shonkin store." In the early days it was run by Watsik Gossack, whose brother Ben Gossack ran the Highwood store. Both buildings were constructed on the simple box plan with two floors, the top floor being their living quarters, I believe. The stores were classic "country store," rivalled in my memory only by the Davis Brothers' store in Fort Benton, owned and run up into the 1960s by my cousin Howard Hanford's two great uncles.

All three of these establishments had a certain stillness and odor of sanctity about them, only one step removed from a church. There were grocery smells mingled with a feel of something abiding, preserved and persevering.

We joked that the goods at the Shonkin store had come up the Missouri on the steamboats. Indeed, if one purchased a chocolate bar or pack of gum, one had to expect a degree of longevity. The chocolate had mostly turned frosty white, and was a bit chalky in the eating, but it tasted like chocolate. The gum was brittle and had to be masticated a while before it fell into line as chewable, but that was true in establishments that moved their merchandise quicker, too. Montana is a dry place, and things dry out quickly there!

It was nonetheless a treat to go to the Shonkin store, and sad when the rural stores folded as the improvement of roads made a trip to Fort Benton or Great Falls so much easier.

Just a quarter mile up the hill in Shonkin was the Lower Shonkin School where many of those country friends went to grade school. I think it finally folded about 1962, at which point most of those kids began to attend school in Fort Benton.

Mom's photo of a rainbow over the farmhouse.

Dad had acquired three antique cars, a '38 straight-8 Packard, a '36 V-12 Pierce Arrow, and a 1921 model T truck on a 1919 frame. He got the Pierce Arrow from Judge Prey, who also had roots in Maine. Dad liked to putter with the cars at times, and during historical celebrations in town, he would sometimes drive the family around in them. He kept them in the Quonset shed, and over the years their chief memorable characteristic became the smell of mice inside their luxurious interiors.

Back in the early 50's as I've mentioned he engaged a hired man from his old home town, Andover, Massachusetts. I suspect it might have been through one of the Trotts still living there that Dad got hold of Sandy Gibson. Sandy came out and worked at least a full summer for Dad, during which Sandy got an old model T Ford truck from the neighbor Bud Glascock. It was purported to have once been the Fort Benton fire engine, but had sat out in the weather for years.

1938 Packard straight-8 and 1936 Pierce-Arrow V-12.

Sandy had a mechanical penchant, and for fun he got it running. He came up with a plan to drive the T back to Massachusetts, and he even bought a spare motor from somebody (Wade Hampton?) that he planned to take along for spare parts when he broke down. However, the exigencies of life were such Sandy decided not to take the T, indicating he would come out some other time and get it. After a number of years, during which it continued to sit outdoors and rust, Dad brought it into the shop and began to do a little work on it, himself.

He cleaned it up so far as the chassis went, and he rebuilt the (wooden-spoked) wheels with new tires. He then turned the project over to me – a remarkable thing to do as I reflect on it. He guided me whenever I needed input, but I pulled the engine pan, shimmed the main-bearings, tuned up the four coils, mounted the Klaxon horn and the side lamps (Dad bought these somewhere – possibly through J.C. Whitney). I sanded down and painted the cab (not to professional body shop standards by a long ways – but sufficiently), painting it red, since the truck had once been the Fort Benton fire engine.

Sandy Gibson with Andy and Pete.

I cobbled together a fabric and plywood roof over the original roof struts, and designed and fabricated (with the help of Fisher Metal in town) two rear fenders attached to the wooden flat bed. Dad encouraged me to paint the bed yellow to match the spokes, with black fenders. For my birthday, he gave me a new set of tires. When we were done, she looked pretty sharp and ran like new.

Somewhere in there, Dad wrote Sandy and said he wanted to buy the T from him. All this was pretty *sub rosa*, so I don't know what he paid, but he ended up in usual open-handed manner putting the title in my name.

I learned to crank start her and to adjust the manual spark and gas levers, to shift the planetary transmission with the foot levers -- one for reverse, for transmission braking, and one for high-low. Then there was the clutch/emergency brake lever and finally the three speed supplementary transmission – with no syncromesh, so that you had to learn to gauge engine speed to drive shaft speed to avoid a lot of grinding.

The 1921 Ford "T" on a 1919 frame with 3-speed and wormdrive.

When I felt I could fly her, I took off on a cross-county trip down to Big Sag to see Dewey, then over to Highwood where I dropped through Robinsons, and ended up at

Dyrland's. Dave says he and Cliff were in the shop and Cliff heard me coming before he saw me, saying, "That's a Model T." The distinctive click of the four coils and the chug of the engine were recognizable to that accomplished mechanic.

I then drove back across the Highwood bench – I don't remember if I hit Long's or Hanford's farms, but I arrived back at our farm exultant at our success.

Alas, hubris enters into so many human endeavors! The Model T engine did not have a dipstick for checking oil as modern engines do. Rather it had two petcocks – little spigots on the flywheel housing. The top petcock was to show you that the engine was filled with oil and the bottom one was to show you that it was low on oil. I did not have sufficient knowledge of the physics of fluids to realize that if there was any oil at all in the engine, each of these would catch a few drops that stayed in the petcock, so that when you opened it, a few drops would run out. And I did not have enough sense to realize that I needed to check the lower one each time or that I needed to see a flow of oil from it. So I kept checking the upper petcock and kept getting a few drops of oil.

My friend Jim Herbold from town came out and stayed overnight. In the morning, we checked the radiator and gasoline on the T, got my few drips of oil from the top petcock, and we set off to drive to Fort Benton. I don't think we got further than Spring Coulee when the engine began to overheat, and I hadn't a clue why. We stopped and got some water from a ditch, pouring it over the radiator, and then refilling the radiator. A few more miles and it was steaming again. We filled it a couple more times, and checked the oil – a few drops from the top petcock.

By the time we got to town I had deep foreboding that something was seriously wrong – and when I figured it out -- I had run it dry of oil. It still ran, but pretty roughly. Once we discovered the oil problem, we filled it and I even took a classmate to the drive-in movies in it! But it ran poorly after that – loose main bearings.

I went off to college and I think it was my sophomore year that I sold it to my Cousin Ron's son Andy, who had his own trouble with it, but eventually sold it for a substantial profit. That truck will always be parked in a corner of my memory – my first vehicle, nearly 29 years older than myself.

As I was working on it, there were several points where I felt God was giving me particular encouragements. During that junior summer and the next one, too, I attended a Bible study at Aunt Marian's one evening a week. There a number of cousins and friends from Highwood read the Bible and prayed under Aunt Marian's tutelage. As I think I've mentioned elsewhere, there had been a charismatic revival of sorts in the Highwood Methodist church community, and many people had come to take the Christian faith seriously, including Aunt Marian.

Jim Herbold & I about to embark on our ill-fated trip to town.

At any rate, things began to "go right" for me when I was working on the T. One instance I remember involved replacing the engine pan after working on the bottom of the engine. This involved tightening bolts through a flange into crown nuts, and then further adjusting them so that a cotter pin could be inserted through a hole in the bolt to render them secure. Only every time I tightened the bolt and nut down, the cotter pin fit through the hole with no need of further adjustment! And this continued all the way around the pan – maybe sixteen or so bolts! I realized the odds of this were very small indeed and I was convinced God was letting me know he loved me. A somewhat greasy mystical experience.

Dad had great affection for his two other antique cars, but he never had enough time to get them in the shape he would have liked. They seemed to attract mice despite their tightly built bodies . Eventually he sold them both to another farmer who devoted more time to them. We have a few photographs of the family driving in a parade or standing beside these cars in our Sunday best. I realized too late in life that vehicles were much more important to Dad than I thought, much more than they are to me. For instance toward the end of his life, he treasured his Dodge Cordoba, and just found comfort looking out of his window and seeing it.

While I tell people my first car was a model T truck, the first vehicle most of us kids operated was the riding mower with which we tried to subdue the grasses that grew fairly thick in much of the farmyard. There were a few occasions where it nearly got away from us, but by the grace of God no one was ever injured.

The heavy advice of the Hanfords really did help to preserve us –"Always do this . . .," "Never do this . . ., " and "When this happen, you must do this . . ." really did preserve life and limb. This was part of the disconnect I had with my children. Farming is said to be the second most dangerous occupation, second only to lumbering, and ahead of mining. But my kids' urban world didn't have the same kinds of dangers my farm world had – so I really wasn't much help to them with my various safety tips and procedural exhortations, or even with my "be careful" perspective.

There was a less commendable tradition that went with the heavy advice approach, and this was the practice of always drawing a moral from every event, be it success or failure, happy event or mishap. This moralistic approach to reality was part of the reason Grandfather could cheerfully recite Laertes's speech from Hamlet, "Neither a borrower nor a lender be . . .To thine own self be true . . ." apparently without any sense that Shakespeare intended it to be ironical.

Our early years of farm life quickly grew their own patterns, besides those related to Bart. We had assigned chores as I have mentioned – mopping and cleaning, and we helped Mom with the vegetable and flower garden.

Mom and Dad built a very nice rock garden behind the house, putting all kinds of different interesting rocks in it, from cocoanut-sized "gibbers" to boulders. (Dad had a carefully worked out system for naming every size of rock. "Gibber" was his label for a cantaloupe-sized one.)

Bin building crew coming in for lunch.

One advantage of farming on the prairie is you get well-acquainted with rocks. Every field has piles of them along the fence rows, or in the adjacent coulees. "Picking rock" was one of the many strenuous exercises the early pioneers had to perform. I had a chance one summer late in high school to pick rock on a newly broken stretch of prairie the Longs owned. I drove a flatbed truck around the field "pressing" each stone and setting it on the bed. The joy of it was partly in the challenge of trying to lift them all. There were only a couple we had to come back and get with the tractor bucket.

In the early days of Dad's farming he had a "stone boat" a sort of a sled made from three 2x12s with a curved iron "prow" and a few more bands of steel across them. This was pulled behind the tractor and the stones loaded on until it was ready to dump in a rock pile.

A new family tradition grew up around the farm house and the fact that we only lived there three or four months a year, while Dad and sometimes others of us would go out and work on the farm for much of the rest of the year. On these occasions, the workers would have to scrounge their own lunches, and as supplies dwindled, these became increasingly odd and meager.

These meals, with Dad as head chef, were often hard-won and somewhere in there Dad coined the title "Granny's Groaning Board" to describe them. The emphasis and semantics were somewhat ambivalent in contrast to the traditional references to "the groaning board," generally taken I think, to suggest an abundance of vittals. Dad became "Granny," with a slight hat-tip to the comedian, Jonathan Winters, who had a character known as "Maudy Fricker" or "Granny."

Granny's Groaning Board had a number of traditions. Left-overs and ice cream, generally served with soda pop, ice tea, or Koolaid, were staples. Old breakfast cereal and canned goods of indeterminate age often sufficed. Whenever anyone complained about the food, say in an expression borrowed from the Pogo comic books "Tastes just like old campaign buttons!" supplemented with, "My favorite!", Granny would always say something like, "Now quit your Joshin', boys," and if it persisted, she would speak a friendly warning, "Now don't complain, fellas. Remember Joe." Joe it seems was a patron who mysteriously disappeared after a meal at which he complained. What specifically became of him is unknown – rumors abound, but no one wants to speculate out loud.

Old Gran is generally a merry soul "harmless when not aroused" (from a Hal Holbrook rendition of a Mark Twain monologue). But Granny did sometime make her threats specific. For instance she referred to the "flip-flops," a malady which may or may not be symptomatic of whatever finally got Joe. She also warned against eating too fast or too much as liable to bring on the flip-flops.

A wider family picnic where Dad led classes in "tickling trout"

All of the mystery helped keep Granny's boarders in line, happy to be fed corned beef hash from a rusty can and drink cherry Koolaid with it. Toward spring, Granny's boarders dearly longed for the day the whole family would move to the farm with a welcome change of cooks.

Dad once got in a fix when he was farming pretty much by himself. He climbed to the top of a Butler steel bin to fasten the lid, and the wind knocked his ladder down, leaving him high and dry 25 or 30 feet in the air.

He stood atop the bin roof and waved his arm at several of the vehicles infrequently driving by 3/4 mile away on the county road. One or two drivers waved cheerfully back. So he sat and considered his options.

The auger was in position at the adjacent bin. However, sliding down its steep length seemed chancy, together with the prior necessity of a three foot leap from one slippery steel roof to another, with nothing but bolt heads to hang on to as one made one's landing.

A harvest lunch delivered by one of several Dodge vans.

After a good deal of thought, and a thorough survey of the resources available to him, he came up with an idea. He had a 9/16 wrench, and a short length of rod with a bin probe on the end. He took various parts of the bin roof apart with the wrench and fastened them together. Using a section of steel strap as a hook, he tied together every bit of clothing and fabric (including his belt) he had in his possession, (leaving only his BVDs for extreme purposes of modesty) in order to have enough length to reach the ladder on the ground.

He dangled this Rube Goldberg assembly from the edge of the roof and succeeded in hooking the ladder. But as he began to hoist it, a weak knot gave way and not only dropped the ladder, but several feet of his fishing apparatus. He climbed back up to the top of the full bin and got inside atop the grain to see if there was anything else he could use to extend the rig. He was greatly surprised to feel something hard below the surface of the wheat. Exploration proved it was another nine or ten feet of rod for the bin probe, which had been buried in the grain! He hadn't known what became of it after accidentally leaving it in the bin two weeks earlier.

Crew hamming it up with a boulder to be moved from a field.
Same time as Great Daylight Fireball of 1972.

Once again he put together his components. Double checking his remaining knots, he then lowered his modified recovery tool and succeeded in hooking the ladder. Ever so gently he hauled it up and restored it to its upright position. He quickly descended, just to recover the feel of the ground again. Considerable time was spent, however, untying his clothing, redressing himself, and reassembling the various parts of the bin he removed.

Thus the story was entered in the book of family legends. A slightly modified version of the story ended up published in a 1971 *Montana Farmer-Stockman*, written by Dad's friend Leland "Red" Cade. More variations told here and there under poetic license included Dad retaining no garment at all, a neighboring farm wife driving through the yard as Dad huddled on the far side of the bin roof, various parties showing up at the last minute and making rude comments as they replaced the ladder, and so on.

Dusk at harvest: gold dust infusing the land and sky.

Another aerial photo of the farmstead, looking southwest.

Art Photo of the reservoir, complete with "Toroto" han.

BARTHOLOMEW

The first summer we moved to the farm, the Episcopal minister in Fort Benton advertised a litter of Labrador pups. All were black except for one that was very blond – of course we took the oddball. The rumor was that his father was a German Shepherd. My first farm duties thus included housebreaking "Bart," that little darling. We asked the minister if it had a name, and he said, "no, it would be better for you to wait and name it based on its character -- perhaps something like 'Piddle-poop' ". He wasn't just a whistling Dixie! (My only other memory of that man was one time when he substitute taught in high school. He was the first person I ever heard use an obscure word, which prior to that was used among us *sub rosa*, (inaccurately as it turns out) but never in public. He asked us if we were "just going to sit here on our twats," or were we going to discuss the book?) We named the dog Bartholomew, since all the other boys had names from the disciples.

It was a cool, wet spring the year we first moved to the farm, and Bart lived in the house for his first few weeks, but partly due to his slow toilet training and partly because the weather improved, he was turned out into the cruel world, and gradually his attempts to get in the house were only a kind of ritual. He became a farm dog, which was really what he remained his whole life.

He was strong, and at times quite clumsy. He was certainly mixed up. I suppose any creature with eight people variously directing and berating it would be confused.

He chased vehicles at first, but he got his foot run over by a pickup at an early age, and revised his view after that, though his foot healed all right. He didn't so much fear as

219

respect vehicles after that. One summer we went on vacation for a couple of weeks, and left him with the Dyrlands. Howard told us that after just one ride in the truck, Bart felt it was only natural that he would jump aboard at any opportunity, and so he continued to take advantage of that mode of travel thereafter, even if it was only across the farmyard to the shop.

First year in the farmhouse -- with pets. Dad holding Bart.

Bart would ride along with his head out the window and his nose straight into the breeze, with his Labrador ears flapping in the wind. Generally his tail continued to wag at a pretty good clip, which was always a delight to passengers or even the driver, due to the length of the dog plus the tail. He was good-sized for a Labrador, although he never did catch up with the size of his feet. Occasionally he would stick his head even further out the window, and this was often a warning that his digestion wasn't what it should be, reinforced by a sudden intolerable atmosphere in the cab. For this and other reasons, we more and more encouraged Bart to ride in the back of the pickup.

His animal instincts had higher priorities than vehicular travel, however. If you had him for a passenger and you saw an antelope ahead, you had to quick roll up the windows or else he would launch from the moving vehicle in a most undignified manner in order to be off in hot pursuit. He had a special half-moan, half-bark which signaled he had sighted game. His tail would speed up considerably and he'd begin to jump and turn back and forth, sticking as much of his head as possible out any opening left in the window.

Bart and our Siamese kitten, Singe, lapping up spilled milk.

One time in the early days when he was riding in the pickup bed he sighted a jack rabbit. Usually when riding in the bed he situated himself in the front corner with his front quarters and head stuck out over the edge so as to get all the benefit of the wind in his face. When he was on the driver's side, his physiognomy was the chief feature in the side mirror, squinting like a race car driver in the home stretch. Dad was driving about thirty when Bart saw the jack rabbit. Dad looked in the rear view mirror just in time to see Bart step off.

There was a big ball of yellow fur bouncing and rolling along in the ditch for a good ways. When Dad got the pickup stopped, Bart came sidling up out of the crested wheat grass looking kind of sheepish, and hopped back in the pickup where he rode the rest of the trip, his eyes strictly on the road.

One afternoon early in the spring Dad was visiting at the Long ranch and for most of the visit he left Bart in the pickup cab. Dad finished visiting and got back in the pickup to head toward our place. He got out on the county road and began to maneuver so as to get into the single set of tracks through the snow on the road, just as Bart lost his balance and fell over against Dad, causing him to maneuver into the ditch! Dad got out and assessed, then proceeded to shovel snow from behind the tires so he could drive out.

Just then he looked back down the road and saw the Highwood school bus coming. Thinking he was blocking the way for the bus, he started shoveling energetically and failed to notice that Bart had departed the pickup and was headed back to Long's. Nor need he have worried because the bus route ended at Long's, where the bus turned around after returning the Long scholars.

As the bus turned in, Dad relaxed, but not for too many minutes, because as the bus doors opened to let Marilyn out, Bart naturally got on. After all, where there was that much noisy humanity, there must be some excitement. So after a bit of galumphing up and down the aisle and some fierce tail-wagging, Bart was shown the egress (a kind of bird which is always flying away) and out he went again. Dad was just about done digging out the pickup, but Bart was only getting started. He followed his nose toward the interesting odors that came from the Long's sheep pen and chicken yard. Dad was getting a bit irritated by then, and drove back in to Long's where they instructed him as to the direction Bart was last headed. Dad strode off to collect his troublesome dog. Aunt Marian said she never saw a man with a more determined look on his back than Dad as he went to collect the triple offender.

Jon and Matt with Bart.

Bart's affinity for vehicular travel extended to the tractor as well. He'd spend many an afternoon and often a full day riding patiently around the field with whichever poor martyr had ended up on the tractor that day. He would vary this by getting off at opportune intervals and running ahead of the tractor. I remember once another jack rabbit offered an excuse for an unorthodox departure. The tractor we had those days didn't have a cab, so the dog went right over the wheel fender, picked himself up, and took off lickety-split after the rabbit.

Soon Bart was making top speed, but the rabbit wasn't worried. Old Jack just loped along leisurely, keeping a short distance in front of the dog. I stopped the tractor and laughed at him a little (tractor drivers are easily amused). Bart and the rabbit disappeared down into a far coulee. Next time around the field, there came the rabbit back. About four more rounds and there came Bart back, too. His tongue was dragging mighty long.

On other occasions he might be gone a couple hours after taking off in hot pursuit of an antelope. Once or twice he did catch a rabbit – in tall grass or a wheat field, but he never got close to an antelope, not even a little one.

He tried chasing cattle once or twice, but he gave it up, largely I suspect, because he didn't know what to do with one once he caught up to it. More than likely the cattle might end up chasing him. He chased cats, too, as long as they'd run, but at least in the case of our own cats, he wouldn't argue when they stood their ground.

We moved back into to town in the fall and he had to learn the hard lessons of being a town dog. Sometime during his first year in town, Bart developed a neurotic fear of explosions. We suspect he was shot once – perhaps he had tried chasing cattle in the hills behind town. He limped around for a few weeks with what looked like a bullet hole in his haunch.

After that, firecrackers, backfires, sonic booms, and thunder all produced a sort of cold terror in his heart. At the first sign of any of these, he would seek shelter, any shelter, but preferably closed, dark, even cramped shelter, wherever it could be found. The house in town or the farmhouse were his preferred refuges, but he was not often welcome in these, so he looked elsewhere.

He quietly disappeared around the Fourth of July or whenever a thunderstorm rolled over the horizon. At the farm he'd come skulking into the shop after a jet passed overhead. Even before we smelled rain or saw the gray clouds coming up on the southwest horizon, you'd know a storm was coming because Bart would go flitting across the yard to the house and stand gazing longingly at the front door, or else he'd find an open window on a vehicle and jump in, or if all else failed, he'd make his way back to the shop and go back under the combine in the deepest corner of the building.

The terror that thunderstorms caused him overrode almost everything else in his character. I can remember once spending an hour trying to get him out from under the back seat of our Ford van and he absolutely refused to move. He'd whine and then as I seemed about to succeed at getting hold of his collar and dragging him out, he'd turn uncharacteristically mean, and snap at me. He didn't want to bite me, but he was even more reluctant to leave shelter. I became a little angry myself, and using a rope, I finally extricated him. I feel almost guilty just remembering his fear.

Bart was always happiest at the farm.

We laughed at various of Bart's characteristics, but we didn't laugh at him. During another summer outing, we left him with other kindred, the Longs, who kept him in a pen next to the garage with the rest of their dogs. One night a thunderstorm came through and when Uncle Burton went out in the morning, there was a big splintered hole torn in the clapboards of the garage, with Bart inside.

Bart was well-beloved despite his peculiarities. Many times my brothers or I would come in out of the field in early summer when the air was cool and the land quiet as the sunset painted up the western sky. Bart would run out to greet us, and someone would get an old auger belt or a stick and throw

225

it to him, after which a very active game of tag and keep away would occupy every available family member into evening.

Laurie, Jon and Matt would join Peter, Andy and me as we ran madly after Bart who ran even more madly around the bins and shop or down into the coulee by the house and out again. When we finally tackled him, we'd play keep away for a while until we were all exhausted, and would lie panting together in the grass until it was time to go in for supper, leaving him out under the emerging stars.

Mom's photo of family with Bart at farm, summer 1967.

His was a dog's life in many ways. We tried on occasion to break him of his most instinctive habits. He might get balled out for killing a cottontail or other small rodent. Although he was basically gentle, his instinct was to kill any animal smaller than himself. We only made him feel guilty, so that he would bring the still body of his latest quarry to our feet and look up at us with sad eyes.

Bart's nemesis – pronghorned antelope at home on the range.

For the eight or so months of the year we lived back in Fort Benton, Bart had to adapt to life there. His formative months were on the farm and that may be why it was so hard for him. He got into many different sorts of trouble in town, mostly involving people and situations unfamiliar to him. He retreated on several occasions during storms into a neighbor's house and had to be retrieved from his hiding place under a bed. Somehow he had discovered their door didn't latch tight.

More than once he went visiting female friends and ended up in difficulties. Well I remember crawling on my belly under a house trailer at the far end of town where he had gotten himself inextricably tangled in electrical wires. He then proceeded to scare the owners of another dog with his howls and whines. Generally, however, he was not terribly comfortable with the companionship of other dogs. Some were friends and some were enemies, but by and large he was more comfortable with people.

He had another bark, a deep Hound-of-the-Baskervilles bay, that I first heard on an autumn evening when all the dogs in town set to bark, howl , and otherwise communicate their communal existence to the world. The few times I saw him actually vicious was during altercations with town dogs.

The final indignity of being reduced to a town dog came every spring in our town. A group of flower ladies had petitioned the city council to have all the dogs chained up during the spring months so they wouldn't spoil the flowers. The best gardener in town lived kitty-corner of us and she didn't care if the dogs ran around her yard, but apparently some did. However, Bart found a rope or chain intolerable. He broke quite a supply of them as well as many collars. He would get back at the end of his rope or chain and charge full clip to the other end, doing this over and over until something gave. It was a wonder he didn't break his neck.

Bart with his customary ambivalent expression.

Dad gave up on ropes and went to strong chains. Bart kept up the routine until the collars broke. Dad had a double-thick harness leather collar specially made by Rudy Lusin, our town shoemaker. Bart broke it in two days. Perhaps his neck finally got sore, but after a few years, he was reconciled to the spring chain-up for the month before we went out to the ranch and freedom again.

Every year the day would come when, the long winter past, and the martyrdom of the chain finished, we would go back out to the farm again. Once again there were all the joys of wide open spaces and wild creatures to chase across them.

Even after winters in town, Bart's basic instincts were as good as new. He seemed pretty slow to learn by experience, but his instincts stayed sharp. He never did learn you can't fool with porcupines. I'll never forget the time he killed a big one near the bottom of the field to the south, while I was driving tractor. I tried to head him off from it several times, but in the end he killed it. How I resented the long and mutually painful task of removing the many quills that bristled from his face. I suppose his agony was greater than mine, but not his chagrin!

I had to pin his head between my knees and grab each one with the pliers, then give it sharp tug, because those barbed quills don't let loose easily. Each time he would yelp and struggle, but I had a sense of poetic justice about the whole thing, and grimly kept it up to the bitter end. In a few cases, we missed some quills inside his mouth and would find them working their way out through his muzzle a week later.

Neither did he have any sense regarding skunks. How well I remember him pursuing a skunk, which each time he got close let loose a shot of strong scent point blank in Bart's face. The dog then ran out into the summer fallow and vigorously rubbed his face in the dust for a while -- but then charged back into the bushes after the skunk. The skunk used up its entire supply of gagging-strength perfume, and still the dog came back for more. On that occasion I had to drag him away bodily, but judging by his odor on other occasions, I'm guessing he succeeded in killing several skunks, too.

On the other hand, he never got into snake trouble. He was afraid of snakes from the very first time he met a garter snake, and walked warily around it in a wide circle.

I'm sure my brothers, my sister, and my cousins have more Bart stories. I suppose I ought to tell about how Pete was driving the tractor summer of 1968 and Bart had finally slowed down to where he didn't move out of the way of the implement in time. The duckfoot wheel ran right over his midsection and hurt him badly. Pete stopped, unhitched the tractor and took him to the farmstead, where he loaded Bart into the pickup and rushed to town.

He met me and the other kids coming out from town and told us what happened. There was a lot of downhearted Trotts right about then. Pete took him to the vet, who I got to know later as a fine fellow, but he made the mistake of telling Pete Bart'd be all right, which he communicated to us. It was too good to be true. Bart died an hour later. You don't realize how close you can be to a dog until you lose him. How much joy God has given us through his creatures.

The string of Montana cousins, only four short of the total.

MORE FISH STORIES

Early in Dad's farm career, the local farmers got together just as they did back in colonial days, and improved the county road past their places – mainly by putting in a few culverts and hauling a lot of gravel. This meant we could get to town even when it was raining. But there were plenty of other roads, little more than twin cowpaths, and field roads to get stuck in under various adverse conditions. Then there were winter driving hazards, and there were the sorts of problems resulting from venture on unknown paths, as in the story I told earlier about getting stuck in a marsh in the Shonkins.

Farm sunsets were sometimes melancholy, sometimes glorious.

Not too far from that same place in the Shonkins, brother Andy and I spent a rather unpleasant evening, the night before the first day of fishing season late in my high school career. We planned to sleep in the mountains and begin angling early in the morning. Well, just as we got up into the mountains, the sun was sinking soulfully in the west, and it began to sprinkle. As frequently was the case, I drove blissfully in where angels would have feared to skid.

We crossed Kirby creek three or four times until we were way up, and in the last glimmers of the gloaming, I came to a place I had navigated in daylight only once, and I had not enjoyed it then. The creek did a sharp little bend right at the foot of a thirty foot upward slope in the road. It was steep enough that one could get traction when it was dry, but wet ... The perversity of the particular parcel of path lay in the fact one couldn't get up a head of steam for the hill, because of the creek bed at the foot of it, plus the bend in the road right there.

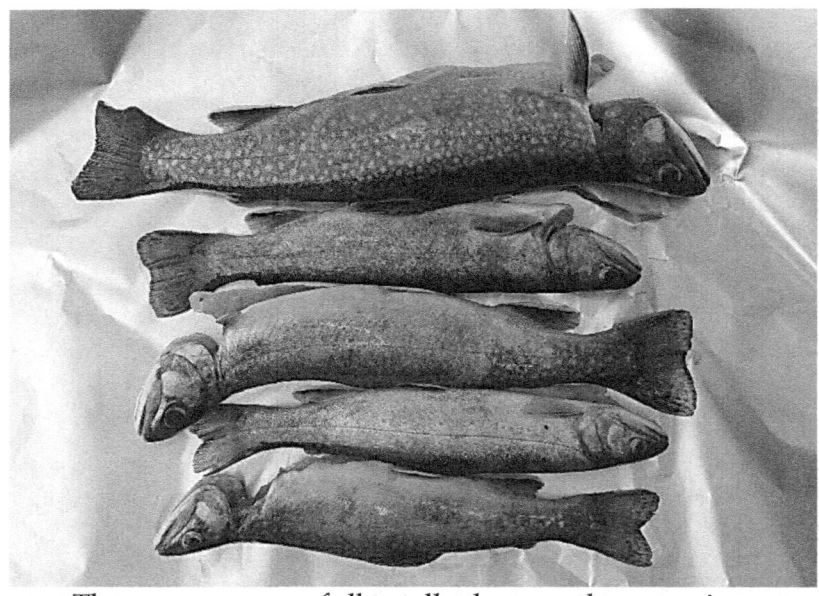

The quarry successfully stalked on another occasion.

So I crept through the creek, and tried to gun the Chevy pickup up the hill, which was by then just wet enough that I got maybe half way or even ¾ of the way up when the wheels started spinning. Forward progress had ceased, so I thought maybe I had better let the pickup roll back down and try a fresh start. The rain was falling harder and it was getting darker. Andy was quite patient with me, but we were both beginning to wonder. In the dark and rain, my effort to back down was misguided, for I had forgotten the degree to which the road bent, and so I managed to back off the creek bank where the road crossing wasn't.

We got out and looked – and it didn't look good. One of my back wheels was waving in the air by then. The rain was coming down even harder as Andy helped me jack the frame up and start chucking rocks under the high wheel. Wet and cold is never fun, but it especially not fun when you're stuck a long walk from the nearest people at night.

We lowered the jack and I got in and revved the engine, but the pickup didn't budge. Out came the jack, we raised the truck again, threw in lots of rocks, lowered the jack again, got in, revved it up, this time with Andy jumping up and down over the slipping wheel – still no budge. Once more the jack, this time some big rocks, lots more, lowered the jack, Andy jumped as I revved – no budge. This went on for a couple of hours until it was no longer a high point among "Humorous Experiences I Have Had," and Andy and I were definitely down and out.

I said something like, "Andy, I'm going to try once more, and if it's no go, then we'll sleep here and inspect the situation in the morning." So I got out, jacked it up, muttered a bit, chucked some rocks underneath, lowered the frame, threw the jack in the back, Andy jumped up and down, I started the pickup and ever so gradually the tire bit, and she climbed up over the bank, at which point I swung sideways and stopped.

Andy and I got out and slapped each other on the back a few times, then we climbed back in, and I backed out, this time over the crossing. We hightailed it back down the road until we felt safely removed from any potential points of peril. There we started a fire and tried to sleep as the rain slowed down a little. I would like to claim it was all worth it – but we not only caught nothing the next morning, but we didn't even get a bite!

Tom Leinart (during one phase of our childhood, he was "Thomas the Lion-hearted") and I got stuck on a number of occasions, usually on expeditions. One winter we really got stuck! I'm afraid, as in many of the cases, I was driving, so perhaps it's unfair to say "we" got stuck. (To be fully fair, in fact, I ought to say that we never would have got stuck if I had followed his advice, but since he was there, "we" got stuck.) We were on another fishing expedition – this time we'd gone out to Lenington's reservoir, which had been stocked sometime in the past with trout. They are fine, large fish and not bad eating, which is interesting when one considers how little like their native environment a farm reservoir is. Anyway, we were going in winter – in fact we were going ice fishing.

A family picnic in the Shonkin mountains.

We took along a variety of bait, including hamburger, rubber worms, corn and marshmallows. (I have heard the last two delicacies testified to as excellent fish bait by a number of liars, but I've yet to see man catch a fish on either!) We spent the afternoon chopping holes in the ice, getting cold feet, in both a literal and, incipiently, a figurative way. We stomped up and down, sniffed, wiggled our poles and explored all the pastimes of ice fisherman the world over, except drinking.

We peered into the murky depths beneath the ice as if to attract the piscine critturs with our shining countenances. But we got not so much as a nibble, not even a bored glide-by. After starting a fire, roasting a little bait and feeding it to Tom's dog, Jasper, we headed back to the pickup, a four-wheel drive International.

As we drove back up from the reservoir to the secondary county road, we were not feeling any great sense of accomplishment, and so as to have some sense of success, I did not take the same detour around a big snow-drift that blocked the road for quite a distance. We were approaching it from uphill, and there was a straight stretch for a good run at it, so against Tom's urging, I made the heroic attempt.

The goal of our fishing expeditions!

Unfortunately, as in the great mountain swamp incident, I made it half way, at which point the frame members became a sled. The pickup was supported on the surface of the somewhat hardened snow, and not one, not two, but all four wheels were suspended off the ground. After a few half-hearted attempts at the hopeless task of digging her out, we struck out for the nearest farmhouse, about three miles away. Night was coming on, as it seems inevitably to do when one gets stuck. Long before we reached the farmhouse, the quiet stars came out and listened to our boots crunching in the thinner snow. Then, frosting on the cake, so to speak, a light snow began to fall.

Under different circumstances, I could have enjoyed it a good deal. Tom had been remarkably restrained in regard to my having landed us in this spot. But needless to say, I was feeling a bit foolish. We cut across a field or two toward the yard light at the Cox farm about an hour later and reached that oasis in that expanse of the "Great American Desert". The yard light, sadly to our way of thinking, was one of those increasingly common self-regulating sort which goes on and off according to the amount of sunlight, all on its own. There was no human being about the place.

Well, the next farmhouse we knew of was about five miles farther on, so feeling on the edge of desperate, we searched around looking for a key. We thought we might get inside just long enough to call our folks for help. In those days, almost everyone left a key in an inconspicuous place for those members of the family who forgot their own. We couldn't find one under the doormat, or in the mailbox, or hanging on a nail in the nearby window frames. I was all for starting to walk again, but Tom says, "You farm people always have a key hid around the door someplace," just as he reached up into some cranny or other and pulled down the key to our happiness.

I called the folks and we stood inside on the doormat to keep warm. Later that night, after arriving home, I called the Coxes and thanked them and apologized at the same time for the use of their house and phone and for breaking and entering. Mrs. Cox was exceedingly nice about it all, as was the norm in those days. I felt even better about the kindness of humanity when Mr. Leinart gave us permission to take the Powers Motor wrecker out to pull the International out of the snow drift where it had unaccountably ended up! Of course, in typical teenage myopia, I hardly noticed that Dad had left in the middle of dinner and driven out with Mr. Leinart to rescue us at great inconvenience to both.

Which is only a small sample of all the people who have helped me along and gotten me out of fixes all my life, while I've done less than my fair share for others. I could tell a lot more stories of getting stuck, but I'll only mention one where I came off in a better light.

During the summer of 1970, Dad and Mom took Jon and me on an expedition to that distinctive landmark, Square Butte, which I had never climbed to the top, and haven't yet. We stopped in the town of Square Butte, at the cabin of an old-timer named Vic Fontana. He gave us directions to the butte in about five different ways and he kept Dad pretty busy trying to remember which directions went with which route. Vic wouldn't come right out and recommend one way or the other, but just kept multiplying options. "I don't know as I'd tell you to go that way," became a regular refrain after each new set of directions. Finally we took off, quite unsure where we were going.

We must have missed our turn or several of them, because we ended up about a mile from the butte, proper, on the wrong side of a big coulee, and then we had a little engine trouble.

Our vehicle was the family Dodge van, I should say the current Dodge van, since we had quite a wagontrain of them, as Roseann and I have had since. The side engine mounts in that model had one big design flaw. Whereas most engine mounts, if the rubber breaks, still provide a steel bracket to hold the engine up, this thing was upside down so that when the engine mount broke, with a kind of a thump and a grinding sound, we came quickly to a halt. When we took off the engine cover, which was between the front two seats, low and behold, the engine was slumped over to the side and the pan down on the ground.

Dad was pretty sure we were sunk and in for the famous march of ignominy back to the nearest outpost of civilization to call in the cavalry, but he wondered out loud if there wasn't something we could do.

Dad and Jon and I found some idle fence posts, and using the longest and strongest of them across a fulcrum made of stones, we lifted the engine pretty much back into position. Then we rigged up a short length of post between the axle and the ground, supporting the engine pan in the middle. We slowly rolled downhill fifty yards, at which point the arrangement fell apart, the bottom end going up and down across every bump and rut as it did. We realized this rate of progress might entail a couple of days' labor, and we tossed ideas about for plan B.

Square Butte seen from the southeast.

I came up with another somewhat crazy idea, and I've always been inordinately proud of this particular one. I suppose it was based on the raft construction Bobby Ritchey and I had employed on many an occasion during our expeditions down the Teton. We had one tool with us – a big pair of vice-grips. I hunted around and found some loose barbed-wire from which I was able to salvage twenty-five feet.

We levered the engine back into position like before. I twisted the barbed wire into a quadruple cable, and we hooked the loop around a bolt hole on the loose side of the engine. The other end we wrapped around a short piece of fence post laid across the engine cover, and we clamped the barbed wire cable to itself with the vise grips. When we removed our lever the jury-rig held!

We worked our way down the dusty trail all hot and tired and expecting our contraption to fall apart again at every bump. But it held all the way to Square Butte, then to Geraldine, and Dad figured we might as well go the distance at that point, since we were on smooth blacktop by then, anyway. Sure enough we made it to Fort Benton!

I really had a sense of God's keeping on that occasion, but also that my mind and hands were of some value after all. We left the vehicle at the Dodge dealer. I would have like to have been there when the mechanics opened it up the next morning. It was reported they were suitably impressed.

Earlier in this memoir I reported several random acts of violence in which I was the violent one! While this was no doubt something of a pattern, yet I was also the victim in a few instances. On the elementary school playground I was once hit with a snowball having a stone in its center. During first grade I did a zigzag around a certain block (costing me about three blocks more travel time) because a girl lived there who beat me up on at least one occasion and I was in terror of her.

In junior high I got along pretty well with my classmates, but the class two years older than ours contained some bullies. I'm sure they are all upstanding citizens now – and in fact became such by their mid-20s, but we all knew they were not to be trusted at the time. Even on band trips which generally had no supervisor but the music teacher, I remember a couple of these guys terrorizing a classmate.

On another occasion, probably in 7th grade, a classmate and I were playing intramural basketball, and one of the freshman, a known punk, started to push us around down in the locker room. After he picked on me with threats and gestures, he turned to my friend. Now I had just seen a WWII spy movie on TV in which a German spy is identified by his British opponent because he used a tactic that all German spies were supposedly taught – to turn on his companion at the moment when they were discovered, and to act like he had caught the other guy spying. I used this tactic, grabbing Gary, and dragging him up the stairs, as though trying to ingratiate myself with the bully. Meanwhile I announced, "Let's see how he likes being thrown in the shower." But at the top of the stairs I whispered, "run" and the two of us made our escape out into the gym where there were adults to enforce justice.

That elementary school gym was the setting for many a school dance and prom, usually accompanied by phonograph, but occasionally with bands. My cousins Denny and Dwight formed a band together with Ross Rettig and Gary Huffman, called "The Mad Hatters " . Gary was later in a band called "Siddhartha." Ross was later part of "The New Men," a Christian group, from the Northwest.

My brothers Pete and Drew (back then we called him Andy) formed a band, the "Horns of Asmodeus," (from a Robert Heinlein sci-fi story) with Ron Doll and Mike Schultz. Drew was also later in a band with Pat Brodock, Kelly Peres, and Mark Bennett, "Childhood's End," (from a sci fi story by Arthur C. Clarke). It seems to me some of these bands only had one song and played things like "In-A-Gadda-Da-Vida" over and over, but no doubt that's unfair. For a few days I "tried out" as vocalist for a neighbor's band, "The Park Bench" consisting of Gerald Aznoe, Lee Taylor, and some others. I can't remember why they fired me.

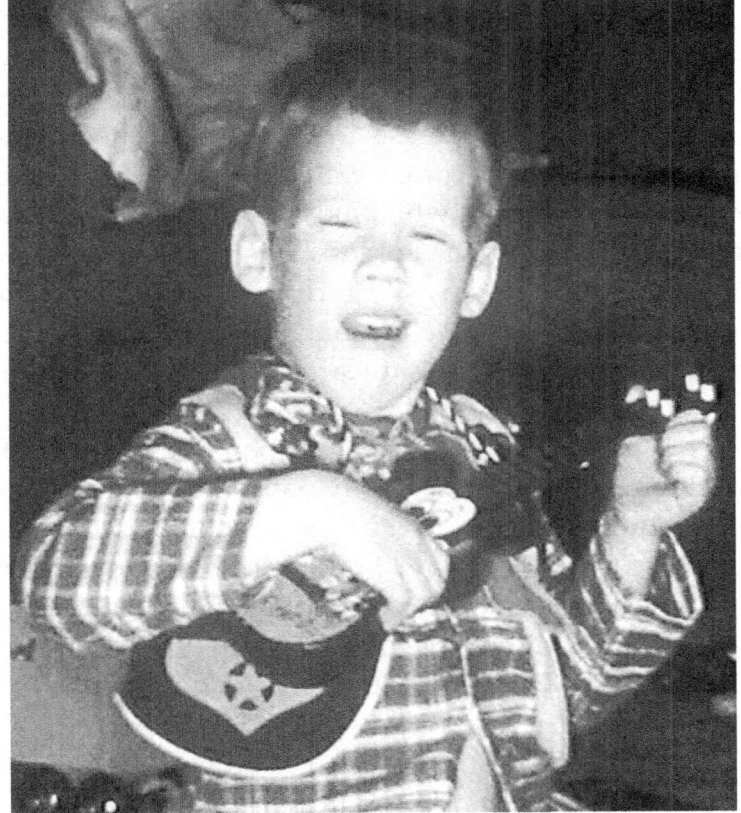

Brother Pete showed early promise as a musician.

Pete tells me Drew had a Vox keyboard which he put together from a Heath-kit, an impressive accomplishment. He later gave it to Pete.

It was always a marvel to me how the girls in my own class kept track of all the contemporary songs. Some of them had stacks of 45 records. I recall them immediately informing me when a song came out, "James, James, Hold the Ladder Steady". They knew all the lyrics, too! My brothers were better at keeping track than I was. Many of the songs I did learn, I learned from them. ("Georgie Girl," " Feeling Groovy," "I Can't Get No Satisfaction," and so on.) I did dedicate myself to learning a number of Bob Dylan songs with guitar. I also wallowed in the romantic and completely bogus implications of "If You're Going to San Francisco, Be Sure To

Wear a Flower in Your Hair." (I had a good friend in college who had gone to San Francisco during those days and was instead victimized there.)

Many of the early dances in junior high school consisted in 90 percent of the boys congregating on one side of the gym (the south side as I recall) while most of the girls congregated on the north side. Only the boldest boys walked the incredible distance across the floor to ask a girl to dance. Many of the dances were open to high school and junior high students as I remember – and thus we could learn "how to dance" from more accomplished dancers.

Once in 7th grade at a dance, Bobby Ritchey not only danced the whole night but mostly danced the Twist. And not only that, but he went out to the Coke machine in the hall and drank nine of the little "pony" bottles of Coke in the midst of all this. We half-expected him to explode when he danced the Twist after that – but he gave no indication of discomfort.

Two blocks from our house on Franklin Street lived Jim Herbold, another friend and classmate, the one who drove to town with me in the Model T. Jim was good at mathematics and I wasn't. But we went through nearly the entirety of our school career together, and had a lot of interests in common. We usually went to each other's birthday parties and sometimes shared meals at each other's houses. However, when Jim ate at our house, he didn't get much nourishment. This was because my Dad always warmed to a responsive audience, and would be spinning jokes, puns and wisecracks enough to get Jim wound up. After a certain point Jim sort of lost control and had little opportunity to actually eat.

When we were quite young, Jim was a very pious participant in the Catholic Church (altar boy, etc.), and since our paths were the same to and from school, we often talked of serious subjects. Going to grade school one day he proposed to me the well-nigh irrefutable argument that since Protestants thought Catholics might go to heaven, but Catholics were certain Protestants were going to hell, it would be better to become a Catholic so as to be sure. I was impressed by the argument, but thought there might be other views.

Clarice Holm neighbor, friend and classmate.

In any case, it seems to me growing up we all felt the differences between the Lutherans, Episcopals, Baptists, Methodists, Christians (which was shat we called those attending the Christian church formally so-called), and Catholics were as great as I would now regard those between a Muslim and a Christian. No one that we knew of ever switched churches. Possibly the only more steadfast allegiance was that of many to the different bars in town.

For a couple of years Jim and I would go over once a week and play cards at the Holm's home, where our classmate, Clarice, and her sister Carolyn, as well as their lively mother, would trounce us at various games. At one point they tried to teach me to knit, and I think I got nine or ten rows on my needle before the project fell into abeyance.

We also had a few parties during those junior high days – usually at one of the girls' home under her parents' supervision. I can only dimly remember a couple of these and I have only the vaguest sense that any of us might have been having a good time. I remember the going-away party for Linda McClain which took place in Roxanne Kegel's backyard (patio/driveway). "Puff the Magic Dragon" was played over so many times I cannot think of Linda without remembering it. Curiously, within a couple of years (two years later?) Linda's oldest sister Pat married my cousin, Ron.

Pat and Ron moved into a trailer in Fort Benton across from the elementary school, and she embarked on her teaching career. She and I had such a disjointed relationship that first year that I think it took us a decade to get over it. I recall the first day of classes. Just after lunch, she was supposed to teach 9th grade boys music. We were a rambunctious crew, although not especially malevolent.

In any case she arrived five minutes late for class, by which time we were in full scale uproar, loudly talking, catching up on summer and about as restrained as Yosemite Sam. Her reaction was to come in like Sam, with guns blazing, and with lowering brow to demand silence. This was not a good intro. Furthermore from the beginning Pat somehow began to think of me as a ringleader of rebellion, which I most definitely was not. My greatest fault was that I responded to humor and irony – even where they were not strictly appropriate.

Thus the worst point in our teacher-student relationship came in junior high choir where we had about 160 kids gathered in the old elementary school library, put together in sections according to our supposed voices. Early on she moved the boys up front, so that we basses were right under her nose. At one point in the early months of the schoolyear during a slow moment when she was rehearsing some other section, Erney LaBarre came out with a really funny quip –

perhaps in parody of something Pat said, and I cracked up. The next thing I knew, Whack! -- Pat had given me a crack on the head!

Ron and Pat in front of their Highwood home, 2017.

This only made it worse. To control my funny bone for the next half hour was pure torture. The only thing I can't understand, looking at it from her stand point, is why she didn't kick me out – perhaps it was out of sheer family loyalty. Later, when she and Ron moved out to the farm, we became good friends and encouragers of each other's Christian faith.

One could do quite a few different things in the athletic world, although we essentially only had three sports: basketball, football and track-and-field. We also had intramural volleyball, with a tournament every year. Now that they have one quarter as many kids, Fort Benton High School has four times as many sports! But we gave ourselves fully to the music and athletic opportunities we had, practicing mostly on our own time before or after the academic class hours. And that's not to mention the academic opportunities!

Gary Gomoll & Al Calkins front rank, Dan Laubach & I behind.

In grade school we played recorders. After that I don't think we had any formal music until 7th grade – but at that point we could be in junior high band as well as junior high chorus. And as we progressed we could be in more and more ensembles of various sorts as well as work on solos for district and state music festivals. I played the trombone, starting out in 7th grade, and by 9th, I and two classmates, Gary Gomoll and Danny Laubach were the third trombone section.

By our senior year we were the first trombones, and that was the pattern pretty much forever. Furthermore by 9th grade a band member might also be in Pep Band (playing at football and basketball games), Dance Band (playing big-bandish old hit tunes – "The Shadow of your Smile," "Autumn Leaves," etc.) or even a brass quartet. Likewise in music – we could be in the larger choruses, but might make it into Madrigals, a smaller more elite chorus, as well. I think we even had a boys' and girls' chorus for a few years. There were solos, duets, trios, and quartets, and one or two musicals per year with dramatic parts and music. Our music teachers and leaders were pretty talented and they worked hard.

Our sophomore year, my good friend Rocky Highfill and I ran long distance in track, and also were in a class play. That was on top of full classes, his FFA and 4H involvement, and my involvement in band and chorus. Rocky and I talked Miss Tesch, the director, into letting us grow beards for the play. Then we told Coach McKeever that we had to grow beards for the play, so despite some joshing from other coaches at track meets, he let us run with our beards.

My friend, classmate and co-conspirator Rocky Highfill.

I'm glad there wasn't some sensitive sympathetic person in our lives to tell us we were working too hard at too many things. We didn't think of it that way. We certainly weren't sure why we were doing all these things, but we knew of no reason not to. In retrospect I feel highly blessed to have been landed in a setting where one could be equipped to live a fairly "wide" life. Of course, there's a sense in which a wide life may be a shallow one, but that doesn't seem to have been the result.

There was no predicting what any of my classmates would end up doing based on what he or she seemed to like best then. In some ways my own biography would be most suitable for the back of a novel. ". . .Then after seven years of sailing the high seas before the mast on Liberian-registered coal ships, the author took up buffalo ranching in Argentina..." and so forth.

Nor did all our activities center on the school. Nearly every kid in the school belonged to a family that had some sort of working connection to a church, ranging from nominal (twice a year attendance) to pious (never miss a meeting). The only reason I hold back from calling our family pious (for we didn't ever miss a meeting, at least not during the school year) is that I'm quite unsure why we did it, and I think a pious person does know. But with all the offices of church organization my folks held and with all us kids in MYF, we still had time to sing in the church's choirs and occasionally take a turn singing a special anthem.

The choir practiced once a week – I believe it was on Thursday nights, and until Pete, then the others came along, I was the only boy. Back in the day, Mrs. Hough (the organist and my 2nd grade teacher) also maintained a junior high or was it "youth" choir – I think Bobby Ritchey and I made life difficult for her then. But for the first several years I was in Senior Choir there were basically three other men – Bob Doll (tenor), Chuck Chappell (tenor/baritone,) and Kenny Vinion (bass). I preferred bass, too, but was usually a baritone, while

Chuck went in to support Bob. As in most regular gatherings of men, there were certain standard lines that had to be trotted out (I am chary of that expression, but one cannot let personal feelings impede art). Kenny Vinion, for example, would sometimes volunteer that we would be glad to sing tenor if need be (suitable pause) ". . .ten or twelve miles away!" He would also offer to sing solo ". . .so low you can't hear me".

I'm not sure if Mae Silvius was our choir director all those years, but I know she was for quite a few. Her daughter went on to sing professionally in Seattle or somewhere out of state. Mae was always training up voices, and had inexpensive voice lessons for aspiring songsters at her home in the back of the Chouteau House. I and several siblings learned from her about opening your throat like you were swallowing a hot potato, and singing from your chest, by which she meant the diaphragm.

She helped me gradually to see that you really could and even ought to let your voice do all it was capable of – even in a world where social relations and communications were always under the restraint of not "showing off," there was a place to really open up and sing. I think it was a great deal due to Mae, and to my various school music teachers, Miss Wareheim, Mrs. Long, Mr. Schreuder, Miss Tesch, and Mr. Nichols that I learned to love to sing and play.

My brother Jon had a truly remarkable voice and I don't know if he broke Mae Silvius' heart, but in some sense he broke Mom and Dad's heart with his decision to leave Gordon College's music program. Barely into his second semester as a freshman, he joined Jesus People USA in Chicago. Jon thought the decision was a clear-cut one. I still don't know what to think, except that God draws our lives with some pretty squiggly lines! Certainly mine was unpredictable!

Andy brought the house down at a school/fair variety show while dressed in an old-fashioned Boy Scout uniform with shorts and hat, he sang "Camp Granada," that comic hit by Allan Sherman which may have been the best song he ever wrote. Drew bowed to popular demand on a couple of later occasions, and performed it again -- the last I recall being Mom and Dad's 60th anniversary celebration in 2007.

But school was the center of our activities nine months per year, and they were more than just academic, musical or athletic.   Although I did not, many of my classmates belonged to FFA, Future Farmers of America, and it was a well-organized and influential club. They were part of a national organization and I remember how proud the town and county were in the early '60s, when one of our high school seniors won a prestigious Future Farmer of the Year award, one of four given throughout the nation.

That was Henry Nagamori, whose parents were first generation immigrants back in the early 1900s.   His father worked for the Great Northern Railroad, then went back to Japan to marry. They ended up farming near Loma.

The school had various clubs, including the science club of which I was a proud member. I think Tom Craig was our president, he who coined the nickname "Tro-pi," based on my tendency to top the final t's in my name with the same crossbar.   Tom also had a 50s vintage Lincoln Mercury with the porthole back windows and tailfins. The science club's most ambitious projects were field trips every couple of years. I recall a field trip we went on for several days, stopping at a wide range of "scientific" sites in a wide arc of locations around the western part of the state.

We visited a vermiculite mining and processing plant. I was impressed to find someone had bought up old gold-processing equipment, including a whole bank of spiral troughs which had holes near the outer edges so the water-borne gold would slide up the side of the trough by centrifugal force, and was thus separated. The vermiculite folks had covered up the outer holes and cut new ones on the inside edges of the troughs, since vermiculite (mica) is a very light mineral. They were also experimenting with using vermiculite as yeast in low calorie bread, since it has no nutritional value to the human body, except as fiber, but when heated it expands to forty times its volume.

We went to a pressure-treated pole processing plant. Few of us had even heard of pressure-treated lumber in those days. One of my farming cousins made his own creosote and soaked his fence posts in a barrel of it for months on end before putting them in the ground. When they could get it, early Montana pioneers used cedar for posts, and some of those fences, sixty years or older, were still standing. Of course that's one of the few advantages of having less than 15 inches of rainfall per year.

We also visited a plywood plant where huge veneer blades sheered sheets of thin pine off rotating logs, and then the sheets were sandwiched together with adhesive between them, pressed together until dry, and trimmed to commercial 4 x 8 foot size.

But the visit that made the most profound impression on me – indeed that shook me deeply -- was a couple of hours at Warm Springs Mental Hospital. We were taken in and given a brief introduction, then more or less turned loose in the general population (the criminally insane were kept in higher security wards). I recall being devastated when we were taken into a room with young children, mostly boys, who were profoundly autistic. Basically, many of them were sitting inert on the floor or lying folded up in corner like inanimate stuffed animals, only these were real people, like my own brothers and sisters. Nothing we were told indicated the smallest hope of their lives becoming anything other than this.

We were allowed out into open courtyards in the middle of the building, and some were able to talk with the more communicative denizens of the place. I recall coming on one of the doctors, or so he seemed, talking to a group of our girls. He went on at great length about another high school girl, apparently his daughter and her great achievements. Gradually some of us realized he was not a doctor, although he was wearing a long coat like an MD's. He was a patient, obsessed with something likely fictional.

I and a few others left early and went out to the bus in the parking lot. It was overwhelming to me to see other human beings so messed up. I suppose I had lived a very sheltered life. On the other hand, my own aunt had been a psychiatric nurse there, and later dealt with paranoid schizophrenia, according to the terms used then. I had on one or two occasions had her irrational interpretations of reality directed against me. She had been subjected to shock treatments, which like so much of our "scientific" treatment of the insane, seems as barbaric as what "unscientific" people do to each other.

No, I think what utterly unmanned me about that visit was seeing so many people in the various states of brokenness, and the sense of defeat it gave me to think we hadn't any way to help them. I don't recall exactly what we said, but I talked a little with Bob Appleby about it and we seemed to share the weight of *weltschmerz* that place brought on. Bob, a year ahead of me was both a star basketball player and a top student. He ended up going to Stanford which Ivy Leaguers refer to affectionately as "The Harvard of the West Coast."

The dilapidated old Methodist Church a few years ago.

THE SPACE RACE

I have already mentioned Kent "Kenny" Aznoe, who is a year older than me. Our moms and dads were good friends, and so were we, with only a few rock fights in our career. Our chiefest enterprises together were rocket science and basketball. The basketball was due to the fact that he had a nice concrete driveway next to which his father set up a regulation backboard and hoop. The rocket science was initiated by Kenny. I'm a bit frustrated by the fact that I've previously written about it at some length, but can no longer find that account, so let's see if memory serves again for that epoch.

Kent Aznoe, leading rocket scientist of my youth.

253

Space and rocketry were very high profile subjects in the 60s. Kent began to experiment with homemade rockets, and got me interested. His first efforts centered around rockets fueled by matchheads. Matchheads were quite reliable as far as being flammable, with the added advantage that even packed together they had space between them for air, and the oxygen necessary for combustion. The disadvantages that presented themselves included the amount of labor necessary to cut the heads off enough paper book-matches to fuel a moderate-sized rocket, and the fact that the matchheads being loose inside the rocket meant their behavior at the point of combustion was a bit unpredictable.

Kent made his first rockets of tinfoil if I remember correctly, and I don't think they had fins – being basically a cigar-shaped tube of tinfoil, full of matchheads with a fuse sticking out the "nozzle" of pinched tinfoil at the bottom. Kent made up several of these for each launch, and some of them performed admirably, flying 15 or 20 feet in the air. I was merely an observer for those early launches, but I recall having discussions about alternate fuels. I think Kent got some advice from the high school chemistry teacher, Mr. Kindzerski, and may have tried zinc and sulfur once or twice. Somewhere along in those early days, another friend and classmate, Danny Laubach, got interested, and one day he showed up at one of Kent's launches with a "rocket" of his own. Kent had by then built a launching tube consisting of a piece of pipe one inch or so in diameter about eight inches long and mounted on a wooden platform in such a way that it could be adjusted to various angles.

Kent launched two or three match-head models and as always we were quite impressed with the performance of one or two. Then Danny hauled out his "rocket". It was nothing more or less than a spent 30.06 rifle shell, packed with fuel, and with a fuse crimped in the open end. The fuel, Danny explained to us, was fire-cracker powder, which was available in thin blocks in those days, which could be shaved into loose

254

powder for homemade fireworks. As innocent and foolish as
only boys can be, we all stood around five or six feet from the
launch tube while Danny set up his "rocket" and lit the fuse.

Danny Laubach, classmate and fellow scientist

I have been directly involved in a number of explosions
in my life, but I think that was the loudest. An immense cloud
of smoke instantly enveloped us and even such a foolish and
innocent boy as myself knew we had made a terrible mistake
and probably at least half of us had been killed by shrapnel. I
discovered I, at least, had survived, and within short order it
appeared we all had! Not a scratch on any of us, but we did
not linger to express gratitude. Rather, as though of one mind,
we instantly fled *en masse* into Aznoe's garage where we hid
beneath his father's boat and waited for the posse to appear.
After five or ten minutes, when our pickets were unable to
detect any signs of law enforcement, we began to relax and
turned to ask Danny what in the world he thought he was
doing trying to get us all killed like that!

Needless to say, firecracker powder was abandoned as a rocket fuel! Not too long after that, responding to the back of a comic book, or similar venue, Kent came up with genuine rocket engines from Estes industries in Colorado, and our space program was well and thoroughly launched.

Kent was good with the technicalities and under his tutelage I learned which of the rocket engines was best for what (some for single stage, some for multistage), which recovery equipment could be used (streamers and parachutes), and how to design a stable rocket. Estes not only sold engines, but also paper tubes, nose-cones and balsa fin material, so one could design his own rocket as simply or elaborately as he liked. We liked to come up with our own design flourishes and paint ours brightly. The stability business was in one way simple, but in others complicated as we found out – again with Danny's help.

Early on – back in the matchhead phase, Kent and I had realized a space race was a necessary part of the milieu, so we had formed separate "countries," each with its own "organization". Mine was MARS – "Modern Ants Rocket Society," and his was something like "National Ants Space Agency ". Early on we decided we would use ants as "anstronauts," because we couldn't handle payloads much heavier – although once more, Danny Laubach ended up outdoing us, as I will reveal in a bit.

Kent and I put together several rockets and went outside town to his dad's farmstead, where we had a major launch. Kent, always advancing in technology, had come up with a launching mechanism that allowed us to get some distance away. It consisted of a launching pad which was a wooden platform with a three-foot welding rod sticking straight up from it. Each rocket had a short piece of soda straw glued parallel on the main tube, which straw slipped down over the launching rod, and served then as a guide at the beginning of the launch. The actual ignition was achieved by two long bell wires connected to a small loop of nichrome wire inserted in the nozzle of the rocket engine, and at the other end to a battery and switch. When the switch was closed, the nichrome heated white-hot and ignited the fuel in the engine.

Because we had a number of launches out at the Aznoe farm over a couple of years' time, my memory can't sort out which rockets we fired off which times. Some of them were launched several times, because the engines could easily be replaced after they had been fired. (The engines were only good for one firing.) As I recall the engines weren't cheap, either, ranging from 95 cents to $1.35 or so and the economics played a big part in our enterprise.

But most of my rockets were single stagers with either parachutes or streamers, which the "ejection charge" at the top of the rocket engine popped out along with the nose cone at the end of the launch. Often a breeze was blowing up there on the plains, and sometimes we would chase the slowly descending rocket for a half mile or so across the fields before we recovered it. A single engine with a long burn might get a rocket six or seven hundred feet in the air.

The most memorable launch I recall was a tall four-stage rocket Kent built with tender care, having big fins on the bottom stage and smaller fins on each of the other stages. It had four engines, each one igniting the next with the ejection charge at its top. It took off almost vertically, but at each stage took on a slightly greater lean, so when the last stage fired – almost out of our sight – the rocket might have been slanted over almost 30 degrees. The last stage ejected a streamer, and we must have chased it more than half a mile before it came down again. We never knew how high it went, but perhaps a couple thousand feet.

I think Danny was along on some of these launches. At any rate, a little while later he told Kent and me that he was moving ahead to a higher level of rocketry, and was planning to give a demonstration after school one afternoon. We were intrigued, especially when we found he had bought rocket parts and engines from Centauri Industries – larger diameter parts for bigger rockets. I think our Estes engines were all about ¾ inch in diameter. These engines were 1 ¼ or 1 ½ inch in diameter and the rockets accordingly thicker and longer. Sure enough, Danny had built a rocket about a foot and a half high with big fins and a big engine. He had learned from Kent, and had a launching pad complete with welding rod launching guide and electrical ignition.

We were not as close as the famous firecracker-powder launch, but probably ten or twelve feet away when he launched from his driveway. The rocket did fine as long as it was on the launching guide, but the second it was on its own, it turned wildly and began to erratically shoot around in spins and curves, banging into the garage, the ground, and threatening to impale us. We frantically jumped and dived for a long couple of seconds, until the fuel burned out as the rocket fell to the driveway.

We began to berate Danny instantly. Hadn't he checked his rocket for stability! No, he admitted sheepishly, he hadn't – or at least, he hadn't checked it after it was fully loaded. Stability was easily determined by two steps: first, you discovered the balancing point for your fully loaded rocket, then you tied a thread around it at that point and put it hanging sideways in front of a fan. If it was stable, the air current would strike the fins and turn the rocket so it was headed into the air current. If it didn't behave that way, the surface of your fins was not large enough, and you had to replace them with larger ones. Despite our official chagrin with Danny, we had to admit he had given us a couple of our most exciting experiences in rocketry. However there was one more to come!

It may have been that year that Kent and I expanded out repertoire into fireworks. I bought nine or ten bottles of chemicals through a supply company Mr. Kindzerski told us about. These were things like potassium nitrate, potassium chromate (for "black snakes"), three or four chemicals for different colors of fire, and even some bottles of acid. I think we had ambitions to make "gun cotton" with the acid, although disappointed with our results.

This may have been back in the earlier match-head phase, however, because I don't think our rockets loaded with fireworks did very well! We launched from our empty back lot, and in fact I think one or two of them ended up on top of the nearby high school building, where by the grace of God we did not start a conflagration, despite our efforts.

Toward the end of our rocketry career, fairly late in the fall, we went out to another farm – I believe it was my classmate "T.C.'s" (Tom Craig's) place. He took something of a scientific interest in our proceedings. Once again, Danny brought one of his big Centauri rockets, promising us he had tested it for stability a couple of times. However, Danny had added a further wrinkle. Kent and I had on a number of occasions launched our "antstronauts." using empty plastic fountain pen cartridges for "space capsules." Our ants had all survived and none had even complained, so we congratulated ourselves in the excellence of our manned space program. Again, Danny thought to go us one better. He had designed his rocket with a considerably larger "capsule," big enough to hold a mouse, and indeed a mouse astronaut was what he planned. This meant the first half hour at Tom's farm was spent with the four of us going around and looking beneath random farm debris in an effort to find a volunteer rodent.

Finally someone turned over a piece of corrugated tin, and there was our victim. We captured him with a minimum of fuss and succeeded in getting him into the space capsule, which was a pill bottle or the like. We stood back as Danny set up his manned rocket for launch, and he fired it off. Up the rocket went, seemingly without a hitch to about fifteen feet in the air, at which point it did a complete 180 and drove itself back down into the ground still under full power! We let go a collective groan. Our record of no fatalities seemed sure to have come to an end! Not terribly eager to see the results of this failed launch, we gathered around as Danny picked up the smashed end of his rocket and extracted the still intact capsule. He opened it and incredibly, the mouse staggered out, and around in a circle drunkenly for a while, until it suddenly realized it was alive, and took off into the weeds! What tales it had to tell its grandchildren! Apparently Danny had indeed tested for stability – but without his payload aboard!

In 1999 a movie came out called *October Sky*. It was about a West Virginia coal town and four boys who got interested in rocketry, and eventually launched a number of very successful rockets as well as winning a national science fair award. One of them went on to become a genuine rocket scientist, and the movie is based on his autobiography, if I remember right.

I mention it because I have seen the movie three or four times, and every time it comes to the place where, after many failures, they have their first successful launch, I break into tears. There are a number of other things that do that to me, but I mention this one as testimony to how seriously we too thought of ourselves as "rocket boys".

Part of our 1966 championship team, the author third from left.

HIGH SCHOOL

My life as a high school student was in many ways very full -- classes, music, sports, classmates, and friends. When I try to pick out the salient memories I find them still too abundant to record, or maybe too many to be easily accessible. They sort of flow together in a haze. I once jotted down a thought that perhaps God designed our minds and especially our memories to hinge particularly on chronology and geography. We remember things by times and places. In that amidst all kinds of changes in social structures, relationships, technology, institutions, and so on, time and space remain more reliably fixed or steady, as points of reference.

I realize the things I remember most vividly were connected to the time or the place they happened or both. Is it not true then, that the best "system" for memory is to deliberately associate what one wishes to remember with location and the time of life, of day, season, etc.? In many parts of life this goes on without much deliberation and works well, but "book-larnin'," our school lessons, have to be learned another way. Efforts to link them to time and place would build up an inordinate morass of classroom and school images in the memories of all who have spent an inordinate amount of time in that setting!

In fact classroom images only get effectively remembered when something out of the ordinary happened. For instance, I remember thoroughly startling all my classmates as a sophomore when the school counselor came in and showed us the exceedingly uncomfortable movie about venereal disease. We were in Mr. McKeever's classroom. The guys and girls were not separated, and the movie was slightly dated. Nevertheless, it made its point quite effectively – nor was there any mention of condoms, "safe sex," etc.

After showing the film, the counselor, who as I recall wasn't the world's best orator, read off some various statistics in regard to venereal disease in Montana.   In one of the top ten best comic timings of my life, when he read off the statistic that there had been no reported cases of syphilis in Chouteau county for the past year, I exhaled as though in great relief, "Wh-ew-ew!"   The class erupted. I knew I could get away with it because I was well known as a "Goody Two-shoes" among my classmates. What the counselor and Mr. McKeever thought I'm not sure.

In music, by my senior year I graduated to first trombone in the concert band, and tried out and made it into all state band. The greatest rewards of band were in getting a sense of what it was to make something beautiful "in concert" with a lot of my peers, and under the direction of an expert. By the time I got into all state band, I was just starting to get an inkling of what it was to "feel" the music, and thus be able to improvise a little. I was beginning to compose songs, and these things worked together.

One of the requirements for Freshman biology in those days was a summer insect collection. Everyone was supposed to turn in a collection of insects with so many specimens (30?) representing so many orders (9 or so). Because my father was so interested in bugs, we grew up with a pretty extensive knowledge, including knowing various orders, and a lot of the wonderful details about insect life. My mother was also a fan. One summer she spent quite a few hours kneeling in the dust of the farmyard and photographing sphecid wasps as they made burrows, brought paralyzed caterpillars to them, and then (after laying their eggs in these food sources for their young) filled the burrows back in and tamped then down holding a small stone in their jaws.

Mr. Lepley the biology teacher, caught wind of our insect interests and put me, then later Pete, to work correcting the freshman collections. I don't recall what kind of extra credit we got, but I think it was academic points. Pete and I talked it over afterward, and agreed it was eye-opening.!

In general I enjoyed checking and correcting the collections of my class and the next one, but there were a number of exceptions. There were always a few kids who did all their collecting the night before the collections were due. You would open up the cigar box and there were ten big beetles impaled on sewing pins waving their legs in the air!

We had a series of illustrated insect guides put out by the University of Michigan, but some of the "insects" in those collections weren't in the books! Some kids had real good imaginations. A collection might contain several butterflies and moths (all Lepidoptera) hopefully labelled as Ephemeroptera, Plecoptera, Odonata, and Neuroptera! There might be spiders and caterpillars (no credit), centipedes, sowbugs, and various other unexpected critturs. To their credit I must say, I never found a mammal or bird, but I suspect that was just because they are so hard to catch.

Nor were student imaginations necessarily limited to fauna. I remember one ambitious girl had three or four little cockleburs neatly mounted on pins. I admit they did look sort of buglike.

Pete ran into a very honest collection. He opened it to find six grasshoppers, along with a note from a young lady's parents saying that she was afraid of insects!

On a much more serious note, one dimension of insect collections that haunts me still, is the fact that my constant presence in the biology room exposed me to something which I did not recognize or understand then, but re-assessed via my memories much later. I saw a faculty member acting toward a high school girl as no faculty member ought ever to act. At the time I only thought it strange. Now I think it was criminal.

One of the more dramatic events of my sophomore year occurred in conjunction with sophomore chemistry and a two-day science fair we held for the grade school. Mr. Kindzerski, our chemistry teacher, was a wonderful fellow and a remarkable teacher. I had him both for chemistry and for advanced math. I was terrible at the latter, but loved the former. Nonetheless, he was a good teacher in both instances, it's just that I was neither by aptitude nor self-discipline a good math student. Perhaps partly because of the interest generated by Kent Aznoe's rocket experiments, and partly because chemistry had to do with things instead of pure ideas, it was a subject I thoroughly enjoyed. For extra credit I grew crystals from eight or ten different substances, and when the elementary school science demonstrations came along, eagerly volunteered to do a presentation about – you guessed it – explosives.

We had to plan all this out and get Mr. Kindzerski's approval of every detail. My plan was to talk about explosions – what was actually taking place, what made the noise, and some of the common explosives we know about. Then I was to touch off a small pile of zinc and sulfur under the gas hood and show how explosions generated lots of gas and smoke, and finally, my coup de grace, I was going to mix up some ammonium triiodide (aka: nitrogen triiodide), an extremely volatile explosive when dry, and make up some sheets of paper with little dots of this compound on them, which I would set off with a feather!

Every year Mr. Kindzerski always played the same trick on his sophomore chem classes – he would make up a batch of this compound, which is fairly stable as long as it is wet, and he would sprinkle it around on the floor of the classroom, usually near the entry door. Students would come in after lunch and be startled when the newly dried bits of explosive went off with little pops of purple smoke. What neither of us calculated – or he assumed I was smart enough to have thought of – is that storing part of the stuff for two days is problematic!

The first afternoon went without a hitch. The elementary kids oo-ed and aw-ed and I felt like the cock of the walk, discoursing and demonstrating. The finale with the feather and the little poofs of purple smoke was extremely well received.

The second afternoon, however, ended up quite differently. I went over to the high school only a half block from my home quite early, because there were some important preparations I had to make. No one else was in the chem lab except my cousin Howard Hanford, who was studying at one end, while my demonstration was set up at the other end. Being of an economical turn of mind, I had made up a double batch of ammonium triiodide the day before, run half of it through filter paper, distributed pea-size drops of it around a sheet of paper and let it dry, which it does very quickly. The second day, I took out a funnel and a piece of filter paper, put them in a beaker, and lifted my flask full of (as I thought) still wet and thus stable explosive to pour the rest of it through the filter paper.

What then occurred was the second loudest explosion I have ever heard in my life. Reconstructing the event, it seems a few bits of ammonium triiodide must have dried out on the sides of the flask, and the mere pressure of the liquid brushing over them set them off. They in turn must have furnished a sort of primer for much of the wet explosive, such that a large part of what was left went off with a single bang.

Howard was amazed. He says it was one of the loudest explosions he had ever heard, too, and he is a more impartial judge than I! The glass from the flask was blown all over me and that end of the lab. The remaining liquid, consisting as I recall of iodine and two kinds of acid, was also spread all over me and the lab. My eyes were burring, and by the time I got over the shock of it, Mr., Kindzerski had come running in from the classroom next door and was completely aghast.

He bundled me out to his car and drove me up to the local hospital, where the doctor determined that most of my eye discomfort was due to the iodine. By the grace of God no glass had gotten into my eyes. After they reached this conclusion, they sent me into the little bathroom off the examining room to wash my face and hands of residue. It was amusing that as I washed, my shirt was crackling and popping from the remnants of explosive strewn about the fabric.

They sent me home, furnished with an eye patch to allow my sorer eye to rest up. My classmates told me that Mr. Kindzerski spent the rest of the afternoon sitting at his desk with his face in his hands. Soon afterward a bunch of extra safety equipment was purchased and installed in the lab, including an eye bath. That evening a number of us music students were scheduled to go to a concert at the Civic Center in Great Falls. I went proudly wearing my letter sweater and sporting my eye patch. I felt quite the distinguished pirate. The whole thing was one more illustration of the verse my friend Paul Bricker likes to quote, "The Lord preserves the simple."

Tom Craig and I in the chem lab on a quieter occasion.

In sports, I found a tremendous blessing in football during my junior and senior years. I had been unable to go out for football as a freshman because of my broken wrist as a result of the swan dive off the snack shack (mentioned earlier in this narrative). I had gone out my sophomore year, only to break my little finger by tangling it up with Tom Leinart's shoelace when I tackled him. By my junior year, I felt a somewhat desperate need to succeed at football. The two years of my football career became very important to me.

The first three days of practice – before school started – were hard. I was not in good running shape, and it was hot. Along with four or five other guys, I teetered on the edge of dropping out all through these strenuous hours. But Coach McKeever, as hard as he drove us, had a very good feel for when to encourage and when to give a guy a break. Once I got in shape, I never looked back, but gave myself 110 percent to every aspect of practice and playing the game. Coach placed me as a guard. We ran quite a number of plays in which the guard pulled and ran as an extra blocker. As the season progressed, I played both defense and offense, and soon I was starting in both positions.

Coach Gene McKeever

Being on the kick-off team was one of the high points of football. The absolute expenditure of every ounce of energy and strength I had, alongside of my buddies Irv McCoun and Rocky Tope, running down the field, competing for who would get to the ball carrier first and thus be in on the tackle. It was a pure rush of adrenalin, brushing by blockers while going at a full-bore run, then diving for the ball carrier in a flying tackle. This was the height of existence for me! I could be one hundred percent physical and one hundred percent smart. I could give it everything I had to give!

The two football seasons blend together in my mind. We were undefeated. I never played in a losing high school football game. But there were many challenges. Some of the teams we were up against played dirty – stomping on fingers with spikes, etc. But this only made us play harder. We once played at Chinook on a field covered with crusted snow – it had actually been plowed down to only four or five inches deep! More extremity, and the additional challenge of man against man at the same time as man against the elements.

The lowest two points in my football career came once in a game and once in practice. The game was our senior year against Conrad. It was the only time in the two seasons we were ever behind – and it was my fault! Coach had been playing me as a defensive linebacker, but although he didn't realize it, I was in some ways very slow-witted, and I hadn't really got some of the basic principles down. So when the quarterback came around on an end run with a halfback blocking, instead of containing the play until some help could show up, I went in after the tackle and the blocker took me out. The quarterback went down to score! This was near the beginning of the game and I was devastated. The whole world came crashing around my ears and there was no use going on living.

We had practiced an unusual play in previous weeks. The coach told us to use it on receiving. We lined up normally, but as soon as the ball was kicked, we all ran to assigned positions along the right side of the field, where we formed a blocking corridor, up which our remarkably fast freshman fullback, Mike Kelly, ran full tilt. We blocked like madmen, and he went all the way! Touchdown and extra point – we were ahead again, and all was right with the world!

That same senior year a month or so into practice, I reached another crisis. I can hardly explain it to this day, except that it shows how important football was to me. I had started much of the previous year and all that year on both offense and defense, and I thought I was pretty good. Coach had us practicing some plays where the ball carrier went off-center, and opposite me on defense, was my classmate, Bob Blanchard. Both of us had only gotten into football as juniors. We were about the same size, and honestly speaking, he was as good as I was. In three plays in a row, probably running the same pattern, Bob got by me and in on the tackle. I was trying my very best, using all I had, and I couldn't stop him! Suddenly this became another pit of hopelessness! And, as only once or twice since, I began to cry in public! I really don't mind seeing a grown man cry – as long as it isn't me! But the fact that I was emotionally out of my own control just compounded the fact that I couldn't outplay Bob at football.

All the other guys were rightfully weirded out by this. Since we were near the end of practice that day, coach dismissed us, and a couple guys – I remember Gary Lusin in particular – tried to comfort me as we walked the three blocks back to the high school, but that only made it worse! Things were peculiarly quiet in the locker room and showers. Afterward I walked alone down the long hall to my locker across from the biology room, and after me, Coach McKeever came down, too. He put his arm around my shoulder and said, "It's only a game, Trotsky." I couldn't risk saying a word. But the problem, of course, was that at that point, it wasn't only a game to me!

Perhaps my greatest claim to fame as a high school football player was my t-shirt. It was an old white shirt with a small Longhorn logo printed on the chest. It belonged to my mother from her high school sports – either her own or one of her brothers'. I don't recall at what point it became a conscious plan, but by half-way through my junior year, which was the first season I actually played, I decided not to wash that t-shirt, on the theory that being "funky" sort of went with the rough and tumble of football – and might even have a slight "offensive" advantage.

I continued the newfound tradition all through my senior football season. It got so I would leave the shirt, soaked with sweat from practice, hanging on a hook in the locker room, and when I came to practice or a game the next day, it would be stiff as a board. I had to more or less bend and break it up, as you would a heavily starched garment, before I could put it on. It would be pretty stiff and scratchy even then, until I had worn it for a half hour or so.

Once, when I was chosen co-captain of the week and spoke to the assembled school at the weekly pep rally, brought out my stiff-as-a-board t-shirt and told my fellow Longhorns that if they came out and gave us as much support as our t-shirts, we couldn't lose. This was well-received, although I don't think most of them realized it really was the t-shirt alone that I held upright by its tail. I think most of them thought there was a stick inside giving it that appearance. When we were undefeated for those two seasons, I tentatively suggested to the coach it would be fun to put the t-shirt in the case along with the championship trophy, and he said he would. However a zealous team manager, my friend Wiley Kendall, not realizing it was a national treasure, washed the t-shirt, and I guess it more or less disintegrated!

I look back with tremendous thanksgiving for high school football, for my classmates, and for Coach McKeever. He died fairly young, but I had a chance to tell him how much he had meant to me. He was like an important extension of my father – or both were important extensions of my father in heaven. He was one of many people whom I look back upon with a great deal of thankfulness.

Of course there were also plenty of things wrong in individuals and relationships in Fort Benton, but a kind of official optimism was maintained by most of the respected adults and it was also obviously expected of us. By high school my friends talked surreptitiously about sex and pornography. I too talked of these things with a few cousins or classmates – mostly as fascinated and bewildered as I.

The outward face of the community was universally moral. But there were a number of adulteries that became public amongst people we knew. In one case a church leader ran off with a woman in his congregation. By the grace of God, they were brought back and restored to the church through great effort on the part of other leaders.

But there was also a respected teacher who apparently succeeded, if such a word can be used, in seducing a string of high school girls over the years. It was not until much later that a couple of the victims spoke out about it. So far as I know, he never made a public admission nor was called to any kind of public accountability or criminal penalty.

But even when we saw signs of these kinds of things, and in retrospect I now see there were some clear signs, the official morality and the official optimism had no room for serious conclusions or pursuing serious means to stop some things that were wrong. By the time I was a junior, I had heard gossip that one of my classmate's father was carrying on regularly with a divorced woman we knew. The effect of knowing this and that others knew it must have had been hard for his sons – or worse yet, made such things normal for them.

By the time I was becoming cognizant of such things – in junior high – there had been a number of shotgun weddings in town. (Indeed, I once heard a classmate speculate that many in our own class were conceived before the parents were wed.) The first such pair I was aware of was an eighth grade girl who married an upper classman. She had to drop out and per strictly enforced school policy, he was not allowed to participate in any extracurricular activities. Then another popular couple had to get married their senior year. A cousin told me lurid details about their illicit romance – things which were probably third-hand fiction. But all this became grist for my mill – creating more scenes for the dimly lit back room of my imagination.

Another shotgun wedding was a little closer to home in that it involved a friend's family. Although the couple were in positions to receive various honors, they were stripped of these according to policy, no doubt based on the idea that this might serve as a warning for others.

Two people even closer to me came to the same straits, and we all felt it deeply, as we shared other kinds of pain. Thus we caught further glimpses of our common human trials with little or nothing we could do about them! I suppose these were some of the things that God was using to set me up.

Then, too, death was a pretty big fly in the ointment. I do not recall any murders in Fort Benton during my school years. But I think I've mentioned a student who accidentally shot his friend while the two of them were driving tractor and shooting birds with a 22 rifle. There were quite a few cancer deaths, not only those in my own wider family. One particularly poignant one was the death of a little three-year-old, the darling of her family, of leukemia. The first local doctor who looked at her is said to have misdiagnosed it, and thus was given a rather large black mark in the community book of judgment (which book my parents generally despised, preferring as I've said, to assume the majority were usually wrong).

Car deaths were always remembered in the Montana of my day – not only because individual people are generally more highly valued where there are fewer of them, but because we literally marked the highways with white crosses, indicating that at such and such a place, a person lost his life in a car accident. I had some acquaintance with perhaps a dozen people, mostly young people, who died in car accidents. I think the highway crosses were installed and maintained by the highway department – until recently that is, at which point some lawyer from the ACLU no doubt, decided this was a violation of "separation of church and state!" Or maybe it is just politically incorrect to remember our mortality.

The worst car accident in my growing years occurred in March 1957, when I was in second grade. The District Music Festival was in Great Falls on that year and five of the high school musicians went with the music director Merne Parsons in his car. He apparently passed in bad visibility and head-on-ed a big truck coming the other way -- killing all six of them. Six little crosses put together into a bigger cross stood out near the Chouteau-Cascade county line until recently. Many families were directly devastated by this accident, including a few who were following not far behind and came upon the scene. All the rest of the town mourned with them.

A few years later six high school boys went out on a beer bust, probably to the Teton gravel pit or nearby, and drove back together in one of the big cars of the era. They came down the wide descending curve from the Chester highway end of town, apparently with the pedal to the metal, for at the bottom of the curve near the Drive-in they went airborne. Only one of them was killed. The driver had nary a scratch. I recall a classmate of his recounting the scene as his mother had gone weeping to the local constabulary insisting "It couldn't have been my boy. He's such a good boy!" Words uttered in the same sincere tones by thousands of mothers before and since.

One of my good friends in school was Gary Gomoll from Loma. I'm not sure if he started first grade in Benton or not, but I have photos of him in third or fourth. His father worked on the giant Fort Peck dam and reservoir project, then moved to Loma, where Gary grew up. He and I were both inwardly timid, although I may have been driven to cover it up better than he.

On a few occasions Gary and I stayed overnight at each other's places. I enjoyed Loma – where it was always our intention to go down to the Marias where he knew a spot for catching softshell turtles, but if we ever got around to hunting, we came back empty handed. I never saw a full-grown soft-shell turtle until a few years ago when Roseann and I were canoeing with Matt and Carrie on the Missouri.

Gary Gomoll, classmate and friend.

Gary and I wandered around the hills and river on the fringe of Loma which never had more than three or four business establishments including a rock shop and a cafe. His mother was a kindly hostess. And I guess mine was to him, too. We both ended up playing the trombone in junior high and high school. His cousin Albert Calkins a year older was always one step ahead of us in the trombone section. Gary was one of those guys whose face flushed bright red when he was in an embarrassing situation. Come to think of it, he was the one I "rescued" from the intramural locker room.

I always kind of envied Albert – he had a big red scar in the middle of his palm. Somewhere in there – around 1964 or so – he reached into a baler just as the tying arm came flying through the bale and went right through his hand.

Gary was one of the classmates sitting in shop class with me while the new shop teacher hinted we would not be forbidden to tell a dirty joke or two in his class. I imagine this was in the general context of saying 'I'm not going to be too strict with you guys except in matters of safety, peace, etc.' But Gary and I discussed this later and we both found it awkward in the extreme – indeed I think the entire class responded in dead silence. While dirty jokes might indeed be told, most of us felt it was not right for the teacher to announce that it was OK and perhaps even to offer to participate! How early we are hypocritical moralists!

The last time I saw Gary he was working as a law officer and was going into a building on Front Street to serve papers to someone. I asked him how he liked the job, and honest as always, he said he didn't much like that part of it. He died a year or so after that when his pickup truck rolled on a soft shoulder one night as he returned to Loma. Like most Montana road fatalities it was a one car accident.

My own family wore black bands around the long arm of memory. As I've said, two cousins were named for my dead uncle, Howard Hanford. My own middle name was in memory of both Uncle Howard Hanford and Uncle Howard Trott. I mentioned losing my Grandmother to breast cancer. The next to go was Aunt Florence Robinson, then cousin Nancy Long. All the rest of my parent's generation but one have followed and several more in my own.

Memorial Day was a solemn occasion. Montana contributed a very high quota of her men to both World Wars, due both to some errors in calculation on the part of the Selective Service, combined with Montanans' intense patriotism that made for high rates of volunteers.

Memorial Day was especially a solemn occasion for our family as we went down to the old bridge where the American Legion fired their salutes and a big wreath was dropped into the middle of the Missouri to float on down, as my mother told me, to the Gulf of Mexico where Uncle Howard's training plane had mysteriously been lost in 1943.

After a little online browsing, I thought to make some notes about what little I could discover about Uncle Howard Hanford's death. He never came back from a training flight, specifically a bombing and gunnery training flight over the Florida Marquesas Keys on 21 June 1943.

Howard in Florida just before he was lost in June 1943.

The pilot of the plane in which he was the number 2 crew member (I believe Howard was co-pilot) was (posthumously promoted) 1st Lt. Arthur A. Steinmetz, who attended Washington State University from 1937 to 1941, majoring in aviation, and becoming a pilot during those years.

He was assigned as a pilot trainer in the Navy at several posts before ending up at NAAF in Boca Chica, Florida.

There Uncle Howard Hanford trained in a number of different planes. The plane in which they were lost on 21 June 1943, was a Ventura PV-1, built by the Vega Division of Lockheed. It was used by the Navy at bases on Whidbey Island and over the Aleutians. Since it had radar, it was sometimes used to lead other bombers on their runs.

The particular plane/flight (designated BuNo 33229) which Steinmetz was piloting, was engaged in bombing and gunnery practice. One online source indicates there was a ship hulk near the Marquesas Keys sometimes used as a target.

The area where PV-1, BuNo 33229, was lost is sometimes spoken of as part of the "Bermuda Triangle," which is assigned more than its share of uncanny events. The most famous series of disappearances happened in 1945, when on the same day five fighters and two of the search planes looking for them also disappeared. Various strange explosions and mysterious radio transmissions accompanied the 1945 events.

Mom and her brother Howard, circa 1942.

Online records show that four of five PV-1s lost during that summer of 1943 were lost over that general area. No record of any communications or distress calls from BuNo 33229 are known.

One online source – entitled US Navy and US Marine Corps BuNos, Third Series (30147 to 39998) gives the bare bones of 33229's disappearance, but it (alone of any source known to us) also says, "Wreckage found in shallow water one year later." No source is given for this remark, and it seems likely it was wrongly recorded under BuNo 33229, rather than some other BuNo to which it properly belonged. But perhaps one day we'll find out.

Five men were lost. Besides Uncle Howard and pilot Steinmetz there were three other crewmen: John Tittnich, John H. Hester, and Richard O. Mainden. A site set up in memory of Arthur Steinmetz mentions that a memorial service was held at NAAF Boca Chica on 27 June 1943. It seems likely it was for all five men lost.

An interesting online site which gives a lot of details about the use of blimps to spot (and fight) submarines tells of the German sub U-134 which left on its ninth and final voyage to the Florida Keys on 10 June 1943, but is said not to have arrived there until July. On 18 July, the sub was detected by the blimp K-74, and the blimp, contrary to naval policy, attacked on its own. It is not clear if the blimp seriously injured the sub, but the sub brought the blimp down, without loss of life among her ten crew members. Perhaps this or another sub was doing its own exercises a few weeks earlier when BuNo 33229 came along – and used her for a target!

The impulse to memorialize our war dead is very strong. A number of years ago, not too long before she died, a good friend and fellow mushroom hunter, Dr. Patricia Allison, gave me a small photo pin and a handful of army buttons and lieutenants bars that were her brother's. He, lost in WWII, was her only sibling and she had no other close relatives. Although I felt awkward, I couldn't refuse or discard them.

Fort Benton, the community of my upbringing, with its official optimism, had quite a battle on its hands when you consider how these dark things weighed upon and colored our thoughts. They used to say the competition between the bars and the churches was very stiff (perhaps an unfortunate expression given our subject). But there is no doubt they were both offering alternative escapes from death – and neither in the form of simple optimism.

I can't write very long in such veins without recalling one of my father's expressions, "Oh, how you do go on!" Origins unknown, but delivered with ironic expression. He was most concerned with the seriousness of the subject and how seriously the speaker took himself. One could go on for hours in repartee, or story-telling, or banter and laughter, but pomposity got brief tolerance.

Dad once said something to me that I consider very valuable, if not necessarily the last word. I think it was after some official had gone on for some time speaking to a crowd at the Elementary auditorium. Dad asked me if I had ever stopped to think ("Have you ever stopped to think" was a favorite introductory phrase) that one man talking to two hundred people for one hour uses up 201 hours of human life and time? If that was the case, he pointed out, then every speaker needs to give very serious thought as to whether what he has to say is really worth that much.

Think of the millions of lifetimes that are being used up by purely stupid if not evil entertainment every day in this country! (Of course and much more seriously, we literally "use up" millions of human lives every year in their most helpless and innocent years when we allow legal abortion of babies in the womb.) But the calculation of the efficiency of speech can't really be boiled down to the number of listeners times the length of the speech.

Perhaps a more positive equation could be arrived at in terms of how many minutes of the speeches are memorable enough to be repeated by the hearers to others, and they to others yet, etc. Thus, for example Socrates speeches as

279

recorded by Plato come into a fairly high place.

The whole crew circa 1968.

One might also add in a corrective for tinpot dictators, etc., by leaving out the short term repetition factor and even adding an exponent for distance (the further the news travels the more it seems to be valued, although this too has its contrary – California's tragedies ought not matter to me as much as my neighbors' tragedies), and of course one cannot allow credit for the mere printed or recorded or televised or video version. And as for internet repetition and memes . . .!

In the end, what we say to each other from your mouth to my ear is the most valuable speech. If a speaker gives us noteworthy material toward this best of communications, then by all means let's give him a little credit. As for aiming rotten fruit at bad speakers, why throw good compost after bad?

THE INSIDIOUS GOSPEL

I've thought a lot about various ways God worked bits of the gospel into my early life. One medium was the radio. I don't know how old I was, but it must have been before first grade that I heard Christian radio programs. I dimly recall hearing radio preachers, and lots of music The hymns in particular stick in my mind – some of them favorites still – "I Love To Tell the Story," "Love Rescued Me," "Old Rugged Cross," and "Onward Christian Soldiers." I'm not sure how much of the message I heard, and doubt I understood much, but I remember enjoying listening. Most of this took place out in our breakfast nook where Mom listened as she was ironing, or sorting laundry.

Formal photo of the Jim & Lucille Trott family of eight, 1966.

There were various Christian people around town whom I admired. How many there were I won't know until the roll is called up yonder. I've found out about a few: Mr. Blummer, whose wife was my Cub Scout den mother for a year or two. Also Alma Blase, who was a good friend of the wider Hanford family and whose brother had been a sheepherder. Grandma Vielleux and Mrs. Fisher from our church, with no doubt a number of others, may well have been praying for me. My own grandmother, great-aunt and aunts no doubt hastened my coming to faith by their prayers and lives.

My elementary school classmate, Mary Beth Taylor, whom I had the privilege of seeing again once after I came to Christ, was from a godly family and her influence came chiefly through the missionary adventure books she brought to 6th grade for me to read. These tended to feature missionaries in dark and dangerous lands, pitted against wild animals and witch doctors, but ultimately victorious in proclaiming the gospel and making converts to Christ. I neither accepted or rejected the message, but I can't help thinking they were part of my journey.

The Cliff Taylor family with Mary Beth to right of middle.

As I have mentioned already, we were a very religious family, although at the point where I first believed in Christ as my Savior, both of my parents let me know they did not believe in him as the Son of God or literal Savior for sinners. I had joined the Methodist church with several of my peers because we were told that was what one did. Yet the idea that the Christian church had a life-changing message was not one I could remember ever hearing there.

What I did get from my parents and my church was a strong moral code and a pretty good defenses for most of its points. Through my father, especially, I also gained a strong sense of justice, of punishment for wrongdoing, of compassion for those weaker than oneself, and of a kind of humility, in the sense of not thinking too highly of oneself. Both my parents taught me a great deal about God's creation and its beauty.

I've already mentioned the strange pictures of grace I had seen in incidents like that of Trygve Birkeland's failure to (justly) condemn me the time I injured him at the old Methodist church.

In late grade school I began to attend summer church camps at Kings Hill Campground in the Little Belt Mountains beyond Neihart. Although I was a bit overawed at first by the great numbers of unfamiliar people, I came to enjoy these camps very much. I met a number of interesting people.

To the best of my reconstruction, it was at one of those camps, probably about 1962, that God touched me in a tangible way. Beside the pastors and counselors, there were also several of my friends and kinsmen from Fort Benton there, including one of my best friends and a "girl friend".

On the last night of the camp during a communion service I asked God to "put me straight" as I "rededicated" myself. I believed that was the proper thing to do during that solemn observance. After the service, for the first time so far as I can describe it, God's Spirit moved in or fell on me. At the same time, others I knew seemed to be going through a similar experience, which involved feeling a joy and peace that was strange and new. I recall discussing the phenomenon with some of the guys and girls later and agreeing "we had something" that night, which we had neither achieved nor chosen – but rather which seemed to have chosen us.

We were, of course Methodists, and had been told more than once about our founder, John Wesley, being "strangely warmed" at a Moravian meeting in London, an experience from which he dated his conversion. Methodism had since been the rootstock for the holiness movement and the Pentecostal and charismatic movements, in all of which the experiential side of religion is emphasized. None of which can take away from the feeling so many of us had that night, and which was of such a quality that even those who "didn't get it," acknowledged their recognition that others did "get it."

I wrote a poem about it the next day:

> There is something in this campground,
> Which everyone should know.
> There is something in the swaying trees,
> As the quiet breezes blow.
>
> The joy of one who first finds it,
> The peace of one who has known
> Are never bettered or equaled,
> For in King's Hill God's seeds are sown.

It is not terribly literary, but I find it valid even now, for the joy I knew then has been magnified many times in a faith I now both feel with my heart and know with my mind. It seems to me God accomplished two great things for me on that mountain evening long ago. First, he revealed himself to me beyond legitimately doubting – as a God who is involved in the world and the lives and souls of people. Secondly, he gave me a taste of peace which gave me no rest thereafter, until, as Augustine put it, "I found my rest in him."

There was one person very close to me who told me the next day that no matter what happened, he would never be able to say God wasn't real after that. Yet within a few years, the same person said exactly that.

From that summer on, I looked back on the experience of that camp with longing, yet with a remnant of joy. Longing that I might recover the "high" in a more continual way. Joy that the experience gave me some sort of bearings or spiritual direction.

Jim Beadle, Pete and Cousin Dwight – on the way to camp?

Inclined to my parents' transcendentalism (I did not know it then, but my mother's grandfather was a Universalist minister), I looked for similar peace often in the solitude and grandeur of the natural world. Secondarily, I looked for peace and fulfillment in the companionship of people, particularly my friends in church and school, and then in the state MYF programs I was part of in high school. However, nothing very close to that camp experience came my way.

Humanity and nature brought me little more than occupation or at times "sweet sadness," as I came to think of the sensation in my heart – not joy and peace. For occupation, I put more and more effort into the work of my own hands and mind –– I wrote songs and played the guitar. I worked on the Model T and carved things of wood. I worked hard in school – in athletics, in music and in academics. My songs were full of "sweet sadness," and my life felt unfulfilled and frustrated.

It would be false to present an image of singleness of purpose, a quest for the beautiful vision once glimpsed. There were several abiding cross-currents which continued to complicate things. The undercurrents of sexual fantasy and lust remained strong in me. Although sharply separated in practice from my real relationships, I carried on fantasy affairs with most of the eligible females in my life. Lust was so greatly an obsession that I almost feared having free time alone, for all such time was likely to be consumed in concocting such fantasies. And of course, the greatest fantasy of all was that this might lead to a point where my desire was actually fulfilled! On the contrary, the lesson which was increasingly difficult to escape was that the end of all this was frustration, anxiety, loneliness, and more lust.

The other great undercurrent, which I believe God continued to feed with the springs of his love, was a desire to be part of humanity, to be close to those around me, especially my peers. I wanted desperately to be in love with a girl, and succeeded as far as I could tell, in a few instances. I also wanted to be "one of the boys" and often succeeded at that also, although even then I think I knew that we were all so insecure as to make any depth of unity impossible.

The summer of my junior year in high school, my Aunt Marian, who I believe must have prayed much for me, invited several guys and girls from the Highwood area to a weekly Bible study at the Long Farm. We developed a pattern of opening each meeting with prayer, then entering into discussions of our everyday problems with loose application of Bible passages to the same, and a closing period of conversational prayer. We had many questions. Most of us did not believe in Jesus as Savior. I wish I had recordings of those meetings, because I remember very little we said, but I know God was at work.

Aunt Marian, who had only recently come to faith in Christ through a charismatic renewal in the small Methodist church she attended, largely under the ministry of Rev. Jim Beadle, led our discussions and our prayer. Under her influence, I began to pray each night on my own, and even read the Bible a little, although I had next to no understanding of what I read.

I went back to my senior year at school with more of a serious attitude but no faith as it appears to me now, yet I believe God kept me, even to the extent of giving me a girlfriend who was a blessing to me, and I hope I to her, although that, too, is not something I can claim to understand. The next summer, with a little more sense of urgency on my part, since I knew by then I was headed back east to college, we once more met weekly at Aunt Marian's.

The only development which I can recall is that I ran out of questions, which is to say, I could understand the gospel pretty well in theory by the end of that summer, and if I had been truly honest, would have admitted that I had not believed it, nor trusted Christ as Savior thus far in my life.

Toward the end of summer, two weeks before I was to get in an airplane at Great Falls airport and leap across the nation to Massachusetts, our Bible study group met for a farewell picnic in the Highwood Mountains. And as it grew dark and we piled back into our vehicles, Aunt Marian invited us all to stop by the mountain farm of Earl Davison, which was pretty much on our return route.

287

As Earl opened the door to us with his broad grin and welcoming words, he added, "You guys are just in time. Billy Graham is on TV tonight." Earl brought the chairs in and sat us all down to watch Billy. Although it didn't register on me at the time, my cousins Howard and Dave Dyrland told me later that Billy was speaking in England – at a place called Earl's Court, which seemed particularly appropriate!

We all listened to his message, and the old longing welled up inside me. When it came to the standard altar call, I was prepared to be an observer, to think somehow I was on Billy's side, and feel indulgent toward those who were coming to the front and believing in Jesus. But Earl put a stop to that. He went over and turned off the TV, then turning to us he said, "What about you guys?"

Earl had us carry the chairs into the living room, where he put one chair in the middle of the room and invited anyone who wanted to trust his or her life to Jesus to go out and sit in that chair while the rest of us prayed. One by one most of us did. I'm guessing six or seven of us cousins trusted Jesus for the first time that night, and I think there were five or six others that did, too.

Marilyn, Marian's second daughter, a couple years older than me, went and sat in that chair and "re-dedicated" her life to Christ. Since I had done all the official Methodist membership stuff, and had been "strangely warmed," at King's Hill, I thought that might be appropriate for me, too. I went out with Marilyn, "re-dedicating" my life to Christ, but within a short time I knew that I never before actually called upon him as my Savior.

I am deeply grateful that my Lord drew me to himself at that key juncture of my life, on the evening of going off to Harvard. I praise God that he would so work in my life to show me, who in the world's eyes was far from a failure, how much I needed my Redeemer.

I would lie if I said I quite understood what it meant that Christ had died for me – even after I truly affirmed a faith in him. I'm not sure I really understand it now! However, then I knew Jesus had done something for me which resulted in taking away the power of sin and the guilt of sins. These were formerly an unbearable burden to me, which transformation I could understand as a palpable dimension of the difference between eternal life and eternal death.

Great Falls, MT: Mom's good-bye photo as I boarded the plane to go "back east" to college.

THE END

APPRECIATIONS

Special appreciations are in order to Liz Finegan, my best proof-reader, despite her hatred for dashes and commas -- Appreciations also go to my brothers Matt and Pete. All of these read the proofs and corrected a great many typographical, and grammatical errors. My brothers also corrected a number of factual and historical mistakes in this book. However, they were up against a very creative memory and so could only do emergency repairs. The guff is entirely mine.

Also thanks to my cousins Dave Dyrland, Ron Long, Denny Robinson, and Howard Hanford for helping my memory at key points both in this book and in the previous one, *Halo On His Shadow: J.E. Trott and His Love for Light.*

Roseann continues to put up with me and occasionally feed me, so long as I put in a few minutes per day doing something other than wracking my brain and pounding on my computer. In fact she condescended so far as to give this project one last read-through and edit.

I am greatly thankful for my children and my grandchildren, some of whom I sometimes imagine reading these scribblings desperately hoping insanity is not inherited.

For those who have come before and those who will come after, I thank the Lord Jesus. As the former prayed for me, so I pray for the latter – that he would grant humility, wisdom, and joy.

Other Titles by James Howard Trott:

(paperback copies available through online booksellers; Kindle versions of the author's own poetry collections are also available.)

A Sacrifice of Praise: An Anthology of Christian Poetry in English from Caedmon to the mid-Twentieth Century (2nd edition 2006) Nashville: Cumberland House Publishers.

Immanence: Selected , Collected Poems, Volume One: 1967-1988 (2003/2010) Oak and Yew Press.

Contingency : Selected, Collected Poems, Volume Two, 1989-2001 (2015) Oak and Yew Press.

Conceptions and images : Pro-life poems with Prisoners' Pardons (2015) Oak and Yew Press.

A Gallows Set Upon a Hill (2002/2015) Oak and Yew Press. (a novel about the Salem Witch Trials of 1692, in which the author's own ancestors were involved.)

Trott All Day, A Compendium : Trotts Through the Ages (2004/2015) Oak and Yew Press. (Miscellaneous historical instances and anecdotes involving various persons surnamed Trott.)

Thistle Dew, Selected, Collected Poems, Volume Three: 2002-2007 (2015) Oak and Yew Press.

Land, Light, Wind, and Water : Prairie Quartet, Elemental Meditations in Four Cycles (2009/2015) revised edition: Oak and Yew Press.

Was That Thunder? A Memoir of Pro-life Rescue, 1988-1997. (2015) Oak and Yew Press.

Cadences and Concatenations: Selected, Collected Poems, Volume Four: 2008-2013 (2016) Oak and Yew Press.

Poetry At the Heart of Things : Towards A Christian Perspective. (2016) Oak and Yew Press. (A discussion of language as a central component of man made in God's image, and how language works.)

First, First, . . .and Briefest : Elkanah and Sarah Mackey: The 1856 Presbyterian Mission to the Blackfoot Indians (2016) Oak and Yew Press. (An historical monograph which came together after several decades of research -- both Montana and Pennsylvania connections.)

The Travels of Apa Oupspi: The Journals Of Huckleberry Finn together with a Narrative of His Further Adventures by Alfred Armitage, M.A. in three volumes (Vol 1 -2016; Vols 2 and 3 – 2017) Oak and Yew Press. (A three volume novel taking Huck Finn beyond Clemen's boy-book into the Rocky Mountain west, with Clemens among the various characters.)

When It Was Yet Dark (2017) Oak and Yew Press. (A meditation on Christian faith in difficult times, such as that of his followers during the days between Jesus' death and ascension.)

Strata : Musings of a Rockhound (2017) Oak and Yew Press. (A fictional geologist elaborates philosophically on his field work.)

The New Testament Elder : Biblical Church Leadership (2017) Oak and Yew Press. (Scripture-based advocacy of the two-office view of biblical ecclesiology, particularly in the Presbyterian context.)

Custom Declarations: Selected, Collected Poems, Volume Five: 2014-2017 (2018) Oak and Yew Press .

Gender Polarity: Man and Woman in God's Image (2019) Oak and Yew Press. (Hot topic of our times, draws particularly on the Oxford Circle authors and Dante -- their "romantic theology".)

Halo On His Shadow: J.E. Trott & A Love for Light. (2019) Oak and Yew Press. (An exploration of natural light phenomena as well as a celebration of the author's father and his enjoyment of creation.)

Made in the USA
Middletown, DE
05 July 2020